LEARN TO *crochet*

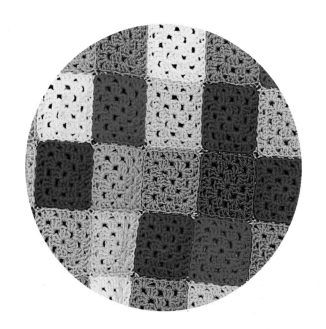

LEARN TO *Crochet*

25 QUICK AND EASY CROCHET PROJECTS TO GET YOU STARTED

Nicki Trench

CICO BOOKS

LONDON NEW YORK

Published in 2017 by CICO Books
An imprint of Ryland Peters & Small Ltd
341 E 116th St, New York, NY 10029

www.rylandpeters.com

Patterns in this book have previously been published in the
titles *Crochet Basics, Cute & Easy Crochet, Cute & Easy Crochet
with Flowers, Cute & Easy Crocheted Baby Clothes, Cute & Easy
Crocheted Cosies,* and *Geek Chic Crochet.*

10 9 8 7 6 5 4 3 2 1

Text © Nicki Trench 2017
Design, illustration, and photography © CICO Books 2017

A CIP catalog record for this book is available from
the Library of Congress.

ISBN: 978 1 78249 432 4

Printed in China

Editor Marie Clayton
Designer Sarah Rock
Photographers Caroline Arber, James Gardiner,
Gavin Kingcome, and Penny Wincer
Stylists Alison Davidson, Nel Haynes, Sophie Martell,
Rob Merrett, Luis Peral-Aranda, and Jo Thornhill
Illustrator Stephen Dew

Art director Sally Powell
Production controller David Hearn
Publishing manager Penny Craig
Publisher Cindy Richards

Contents

Introduction

Learning to crochet is one of life's joys. I heard on the radio (so it must be true), that there is no such thing as an unhappy crafter—and what better craft to learn than crochet.

In this book we have a collection of great projects that are not only perfect for the beginner to tackle, but the designs are fabulous too and will keep even the most experienced crocheter happy. We have a range of pretty hats, fingerless gloves, simple headbands, some really great bags and purses, and one of my favorite scarves, made out of big and bold granny squares. We also have the popular "Springtime Throw" with such delicious colors and dainty squares you'll want to make it at any time of year.

The detailed techniques section guides you through the stitches and techniques with step-by-step instructions and illustrations that are comprehensive and easy to follow.

Learn to Crochet will send you flying into your new-found hobby with confidence and pride that I know will give you great pleasure.

Equipment

You don't need a lot of equipment to make the projects in this book, but if you are new to crochet, the information here will help you make sure you've got everything you need before you begin.

YARN

The yarn type and shades used are listed for each pattern. For projects which only require small amounts of yarn you may choose to use some from your yarn stash instead. If you want to use a different yarn from the one in the pattern, use the information given about the yarn (weight, material, length per ball, weight of ball) to find a suitable substitute, or ask at your local yarn store.

CROCHET HOOKS

Crochet hooks come in a variety of sizes and you'll be guided by the pattern and the thickness of yarn as to which size you need. If you find that your stitches are too loose or too tight, try experimenting with a slightly smaller or larger hook. If you are purchasing your first hook for practice, then use a double-knitting weight yarn and a US size G/6 (4mm) crochet hook. Whichever type of hook you choose, it's important that it has a good smooth tip, and it's worth trying out different brands to see which you like best before making a purchase. I keep my hooks in a hook holder so I don't lose them, or in an old-fashioned wooden pencil stand where they are easily accessible.

OTHER EQUIPMENT

STITCH MARKERS

These are used to mark the first stitch of every round. You can buy different types, but I find that a length of contrasting crochet cotton or thin yarn also works really well—it is easy to weave it in and out of each round and it doesn't get in your way—or try using a safety pin. At the end of a completed round, loop the stitch marker through the loop on the hook thus marking your first stitch of the next round. Counting your stitches after each round helps to make sure you are completing the correct number.

YARN SEWING NEEDLES

These come in various sizes, but all have large eyes for easy threading of yarn, and a blunt end which will not split the stitches when you are sewing up your work.

SHARP SCISSORS

You will need these for cutting yarn after finishing a piece and when sewing up. It is tempting to break yarn with your hands, but this can pull the stitches out of shape.

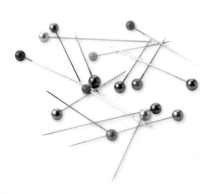

TAPE MEASURE

A tape measure is an inexpensive and essential tool for a crocheter. You will need it to measure your crochet pieces and your gauge squares.

PINS

I always pin my crochet pieces together before I sew them up or make a crochet seam. Rustproof, glass-headed or T-headed quilter's pins can be used to pin crocheted pieces together. Bright-colored tops make it easy to spot the pins against the crocheted fabric, so you don't leave any behind!

Techniques

In this section there are instructions for all the basic crochet techniques you will need to make the projects in this book. If you can't find the recommended yarn for a project, you can substitute a different yarn of the same type (so another worsted to replace a worsted, or a light worsted to replace a light worsted), but you will need to check the gauge carefully.

Holding the hook

Pen position Pick up your hook as though you are picking up a pen or pencil. Keeping the hook held loosely between your fingers and thumb, turn your hand so that the palm is facing up and the hook is balanced in your hand and resting in the space between your index finger and your thumb.

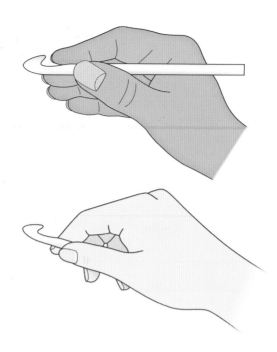

Knife position But if I'm using a very large hook and chunky yarn, then I may sometimes change and use the knife position. I crochet a lot and I've learned that it's important to take care not to damage your arm or shoulder by being too tense. Make sure you're always relaxed when crocheting and take breaks.

Holding the yarn

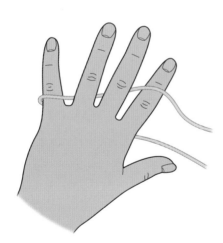

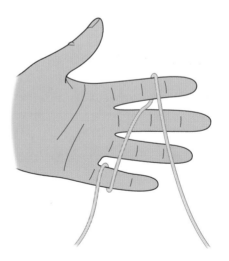

1 Pick up the yarn with your little finger in the opposite hand to your hook, with your palm facing upward and with the short end in front. Turn your hand to face downward, with the yarn on top of your index finger and under the other two fingers and wrapped right around the little finger, as shown above.

2 Turn your hand to face you, ready to hold the work in your middle finger and thumb. Keeping your index finger only at a slight curve, hold the work or the slip knot using the same hand, between your middle finger and your thumb and just below the crochet hook and loop/s on the hook.

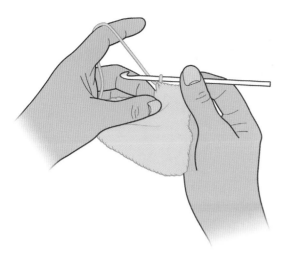

Holding your hook, yarn, and crochet

Keep your index finger, with the yarn draped over it, at a slight curve, and hold your work (or the slip knot) using the same hand, between your middle finger and your thumb and just below the crochet hook and the loop/s on the hook.

As you draw the loop through the hook, release the yarn on the index finger to allow the loop to stay loose on the hook. If you tense your index finger, the yarn will become too tight and pull the loop on the hook too tight for you to draw the yarn through.

Some left-handers learn to crochet like right-handers, but others learn with everything reversed—with the hook in the left hand and the yarn in the right.

Yarn over hook (yoh)

To create a stitch, catch the yarn from behind with the hook pointing upward. As you gently pull the yarn through the loop on the hook, turn the hook so it faces downward and slide the yarn through the loop. The loop on the hook should be kept loose enough for the hook to slide through easily.

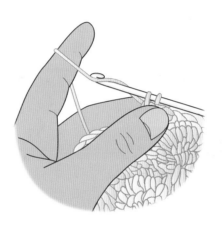

Making a slip knot

The simplest way is to make a circle with the yarn, so that the loop is facing downward.

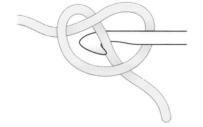

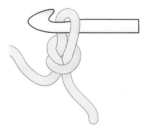

1 Make a circle of yarn as shown.

2 In one hand hold the circle at the top where the yarn crosses, and let the tail drop down at the back so that it falls across the center of the loop. With your free hand or the tip of a crochet hook, pull a loop through the circle.

3 Put the hook into the loop and pull gently so that it forms a loose loop on the hook.

Chain (ch)

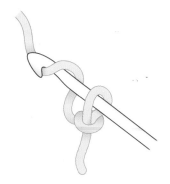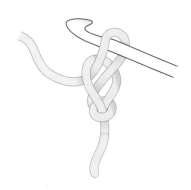

1 Make a slip knot and put it on the hook. Using the hook, wrap the yarn over the hook ready to pull it through the loop on the hook.

2 Pull through, creating a new loop on the hook. Continue in this way to create a chain of the required length.

Chain ring

If you are crocheting a round shape, one way of starting off is by crocheting a number of chains following the instructions in your pattern, and then joining them into a circle.

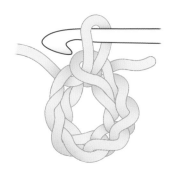

1 To join the chain into a circle, insert the crochet hook into the first chain that you made (not into the slip knot), yarn over hook.

2 Pull the yarn through the chain and through the loop on your hook at the same time, thereby creating a slip stitch and forming a circle. You now have a chain ring ready to work stitches into as instructed in the pattern.

Chain space (ch sp)

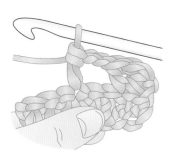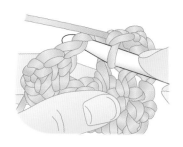

1 A chain space is the space that has been made under a chain in the previous round or row, and falls in between other stitches.

2 Stitches into a chain space are made directly into the hole/space created under the chain and not into the chain stitches themselves.

Working into a ring

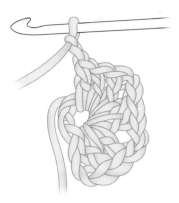

1 After making the chain ring you'll be instructed to make a number of chains to bring your work up to the right height for the first stitch of the first round.

2 Keep an eye on where the center of the ring is. I usually stick my finger into the hole to define it—this can be neatened up later when sewing in ends.

3 As you are making the stitches and chains to create this first round you may feel that you are running out of space in the ring. If so, ease the stitches round so they are more bunched up, which will give you more space in the ring, and take care not to make your new stitches over the top of the first stitches or chains made in this round.

Slip stitch (ss)

A slip stitch doesn't create any height and is often used as the last stitch to create a smooth and even round or row.

1 To make a slip stitch: first put the hook through the work, yarn over hook.

2 Pull the yarn through both the work and through the loop on the hook at the same time, so you will have 1 loop on the hook.

Making rounds

When working in rounds the work is not turned, so you are always working from one side. Depending on the pattern you are working, a "round" can be made into a square. Some rounds are started by making one or more chains to create the height you need for the stitch you are working:

Single crochet = 1 chain
Half double crochet = 2 chains
Double crochet = 3 chains

Work the required stitches to complete the round. At the end of the round, slip stitch into the top of the chain to close the round.

Making rows

When making straight rows you turn the work at the end of each row and make a turning chain to create the height you need for the stitch you are working with, as for making rounds.

Single crochet = 1 chain
Half double crochet = 2 chains
Double crochet = 3 chains

Working in rounds

When working crochet in rounds, you join each round with a slip stitch (see page 15). After completing the base ring, place a stitch marker to denote the beginning of the round. When you've made a round and reached the point where the stitch marker is, work this stitch, take out the stitch marker from the previous round and put it back into the first stitch/chain of the new round. A safety pin makes a good stitch marker.

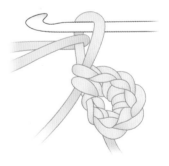

Working in spirals

Another way of working in rounds is by continuing to crochet at the end of each round without joining, which creates a spiral.

 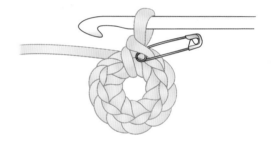

1 Spirals are started by making 2 chains and then making a group of stitches into the second ch from the hook, which creates a fan effect and is the beginning of the spiral.

2 Insert a strand of contrast yarn as a stitch marker in the loop on the hook when you have finished making the first stitches, to mark the beginning of the round. Pop the strands of the stitch marker to sit at the back of the loop—or you can use a commercial bought stitch marker (see page 9). The start of the round will be made into the first stitch.

Joining new yarn at the end of a row or round

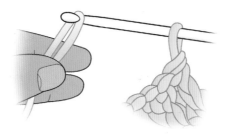

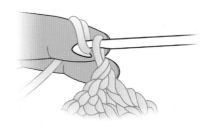

1 Do not fasten off, but keep the loop of the old yarn on the hook. Drop the tail and catch a loop of the strand of the new yarn with the crochet hook.

2 Pull the new yarn through the loop on the hook, keeping the old loop drawn tight.

Joining in the middle of a row

Sometimes you will need to join in a new yarn in the middle of the row, either because the yarn has run out and you need to use the same color but with a new ball, or when instructed in the pattern to change color. In this case you work part of the stitch in the old yarn and then switch to the new yarn to complete it, as explained in the instructions below for joining a new yarn in single crochet.

Joining new yarn in single crochet

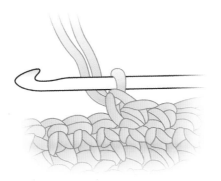

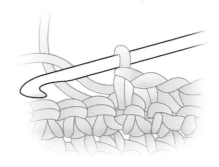

1 Make a single crochet stitch as usual, but do not complete the stitch. When there are 2 loops remaining on the hook, drop the old yarn, catch the new yarn with the hook and pull it through these 2 loops to complete the stitch.

2 Continue to crochet with the new yarn. Cut the strand of the old yarn about 6in (15cm) from the crochet and leave it to drop at the back of the work so you can sew this end in later.

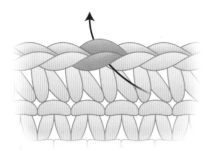

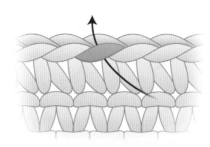

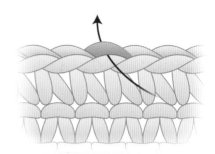

Working into top of stitch

Unless otherwise directed, insert the hook under both of the 2 loops on top of the stitch—this is the standard technique.

Working into front loop of stitch (FLO)

To work into the front loop of a stitch, pick up the front loop only from underneath at the front of the work.

Working into back loop of stitch (BLO)

To work into the back loop of the stitch, insert the hook between the front and the back loop, picking up the back loop only from the front of the work.

How to measure a gauge square

Using the hook and the yarn recommended in the pattern, make a number of chains to measure approximately 6in (15cm). Working in the stitch pattern given for the gauge measurements, work enough rows to form a square. Fasten off.

Take a ruler, place it horizontally across the square, and using pins, mark a 4in (10cm) area. Repeat vertically to form a 4in (10cm) square on the fabric.

Count the number of stitches across, and the number of rows within the square, and compare against the gauge given in the pattern.

If your numbers match the pattern then use this size hook and yarn for your project. If you have more stitches, then your gauge is tighter than recommended and you need to use a larger hook. If you have fewer stitches, then your gauge is looser and you will need a smaller hook.

Make gauge squares using different size hooks until you have matched the gauge in the pattern, and use this hook to make the project.

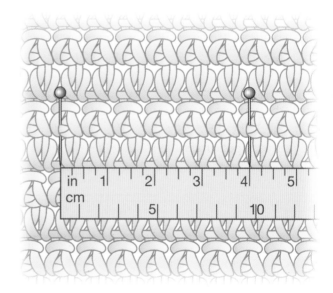

Single crochet (sc)

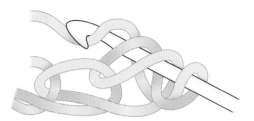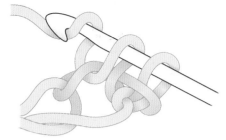

1 Insert the hook into your work, yarn over hook and pull the yarn through the work only. You will then have 2 loops on the hook.

2 Yarn over hook again and pull through the 2 loops on the hook. You will then have 1 loop left on the hook.

Half double crochet (hdc)

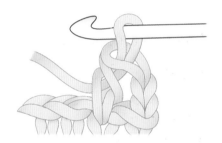

1 Before inserting the hook into the work, wrap the yarn over the hook and put the hook through the work with the yarn wrapped around.

2 Yarn over hook again and pull through the first loop on the hook. You now have 3 loops on the hook.

3 Yarn over hook and pull the yarn through all 3 loops. You will be left with 1 loop on the hook.

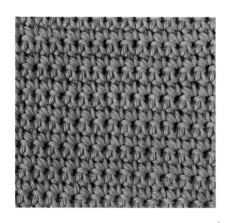

Single crochet

Half double crochet

Double crochet—see page 20

Double crochet (dc)

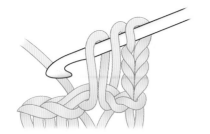  

1 Before inserting the hook into the work, wrap the yarn over the hook. Put the hook through the work with the yarn wrapped around, yarn over hook again and pull through the first loop on the hook. You now have 3 loops on the hook.

2 Yarn over hook again, pull the yarn through the first 2 loops on the hook. You now have 2 loops on the hook.

3 Pull the yarn through 2 loops again. You will be left with 1 loop on the hook. The height of each stitch is called a "post."

Double treble (dtr)

Double trebles are "tall" stitches and are an extension on the basic treble stitch. They need a turning chain of 5 chains.

1 Yarn over hook three times, insert the hook into the stitch or space.

2 Yarn over hook, pull the yarn through the work (5 loops on hook).

3 Yarn over hook, pull the yarn through the first 2 loops on the hook (4 loops on hook).

 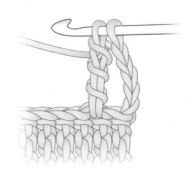 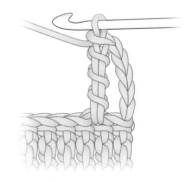

4 Yarn over hook, pull the yarn through the first 2 loops on the hook (3 loops on hook).

5 Yarn over hook, pull the yarn through the first 2 loops on the hook (2 loops on hook).

6 Yarn over hook, pull the yarn through 2 loops on the hook. You will be left with 1 loop on hook.

Increasing

Make two or three stitches into one stitch or space from the previous row. The illustration shows a double crochet increase being made.

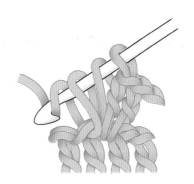

Decreasing

You can decrease by either skipping the next stitch and continuing to crochet, or by crocheting two or more stitches together. The basic technique for crocheting stitches together is the same, no matter which stitch you are using. The following example shows sc2tog.

Single crochet two stitches together (sc2tog)

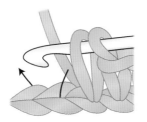
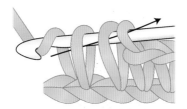

1 Insert the hook into your work, yarn over hook and pull the yarn through the work (2 loops on hook). Insert the hook in next stitch, yarn over hook and pull the yarn through (3 loops on hook).

2 Yarn over hook again and pull through all 3 loops on the hook. You will then have 1 loop left on the hook.

Half double crochet two stitches together (hdc2tog)

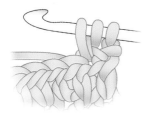
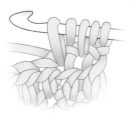

1 Yarn over hook, insert the hook into the next stitch or space as instructed in the pattern, yarn over hook, pull the yarn through the work (3 loops on hook).

2 Yarn over hook, insert the hook into the next stitch, yarn over hook, pull the yarn through the work (5 loops on hook).

3 Yarn over hook, pull the yarn through all 5 loops on the hook. You will then have 1 loop left on the hook.

Half double crochet cluster (hdcCL)

To make a half double crochet cluster, follow the steps above for hdc2tog, but in step 2, insert the hook into the same stitch or space as in step 1.

Double crochet two stitches together (dc2tog)

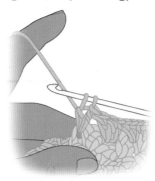

1 Yarn over hook, insert the hook into the next space, yarn over hook, pull the yarn through the work (3 loops on hook).

2 Yarn over hook, pull the yarn through 2 loops on the hook (2 loops on hook).

3 Yarn over hook, insert the hook into the next space (in the next square).

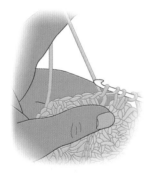

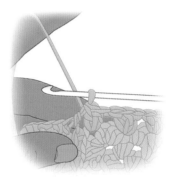

4 Yarn over hook, pull the yarn through the work (4 loops on hook).

5 Yarn over hook, pull the yarn through 2 loops on the hook (3 loops on hook).

6 Yarn over hook, pull the yarn through all 3 loops on the hook (1 loop on hook). One double crochet 2 stitches together (decrease) made.

Popcorn stitch (PC)

This kind of bobble is made from complete stitches. The example shows four double crochet worked in a chain space and taken together, but a bobble can be placed in any stitch and be made up of any practical number or combination of stitches.

1 Inserting the hook in the same place each time, work 4 complete double crochet.

2 Slip the hook out of the last loop. Insert the hook into the top of the first double crochet made, then back into the last loop again.

3 Yarn over hook and pull yarn through the loop and the stitch.

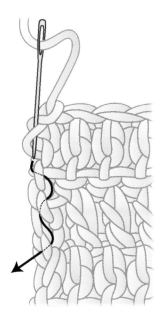

Fastening off and weaving in yarn ends

Fastening off is important to stop your work from unraveling. Cut the yarn first, leaving a tail end of about 4–6in (10–15cm), then thread the end through the stitch loop. Pull the tail end firmly to tighten the loop. You will then need to weave in all the ends of yarn so that they are neat and secure. Thread a yarn sewing needle with the tail end. On the wrong side, take the needle through the crochet one stitch down on the edge, then take it through the stitches, working in a gentle zigzag. Work through four or five stitches then return in the opposite direction. Remove the needle, pull the crochet gently to stretch it, and trim the end.

Blocking

Crochet can tend to curl so to make flat pieces stay flat you may need to block them. Pin the piece out to the correct size and shape on the ironing board, then cover with a cloth and press or steam gently (depending on the type of yarn) and allow to dry completely.

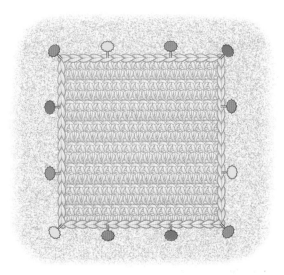

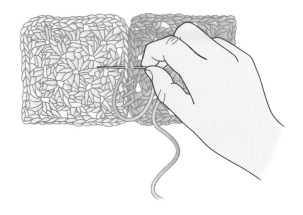

Sewing up

Whip Stitch: Sewing up crochet fabric can be done in many ways, but using a whip stitch is the easiest. However, you will be able to see the stitches clearly, so use a matching yarn. Lay the two pieces to be joined next to each other with right sides facing upward. Secure the yarn to one piece. Insert the needle into the front of one piece of fabric, then up from the back of the adjoining fabric. Repeat along the seam.

Making a single crochet seam

With a single crochet seam you join two pieces together using a crochet hook and working a single crochet stitch through both pieces, instead of sewing them together with a tail of yarn and a yarn sewing needle. This makes a quick and strong seam and gives a slightly raised finish to the edging. For a less raised seam, follow the same basic technique, but work each stitch in slip stitch rather than single crochet.

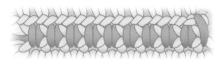

1 Start by lining up the two pieces with wrong sides together. Insert the hook in the top 2 loops of the stitch of the first piece, then into the corresponding stitch on the second piece.

2 Complete the single crochet stitch as normal and continue on next stitches as directed in the pattern. This gives a raised effect if the single crochet stitches are made on the right side of the work.

3 You can work with the wrong side of the work facing (with the pieces right side facing) if you don't want this effect and it still creates a good strong join.

Tassels and fringes

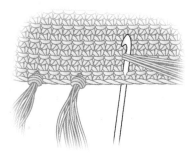

1 Cut yarn strands to the quantity and length given in the pattern. Take a small bundle of strands and fold them in half. With the right side of the project facing, insert a crochet hook from the wrong side through one of the edge stitches. Catch the bunch of strands with the hook at the fold point.

2 Pull through to make a big loop and, using your fingers, pull the tails of the bunch of strands through the loop.

3 Pull on the tails to tighten the loop firmly to secure the tassel.

Lining a bag with fabric

It's not always necessary to line a crochet bag, but in some projects you will need to make a lining. Specific instructions are given in the projects, but the general method is given here.

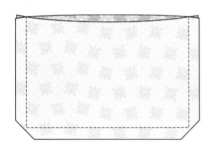

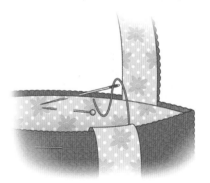

1 Cut two pieces of lining fabric to the same size as the bag plus an extra ⅝in (1.5cm) allowance for seams on the sides and bottom and an extra 1in (2.5cm) at the top. Pin the fabric pieces right sides together and machine sew the side and bottom seams. Trim across the bottom corners and press out the seams.

2 Turn the top edge of the lining over to the wrong side by 1in (2.5cm) and press.

3 Insert the lining into the bag with wrong sides of crochet and lining together and pin in place around the top edge. Hand-sew the lining to the crocheted piece around the top edge, stitching across the handles if they are being inserted between the lining and the bag.

Edgings

For flat pieces, you can crochet around the edges to create a border. A single crochet edging is the base for most decorative edgings and neatens up the sides of crochet really well. It can also be used to make a frame in a contrasting color to create a good effect. Single crochet edgings usually start at a corner and you will be instructed in the pattern where to join the yarn. There are usually 2 or 3 stitches made in the corner to create the corner shape, then you will be instructed to make single crochet stitches along the edge to the next corner, and so on until you have worked single crochet around the whole piece. A single crochet edging is usually worked on the right side of the work. You can use double crochet stitches in the same way. Once you have worked the whole way around the piece, you will need to join your edging with a slip stitch.

Joining edging with a slip stitch

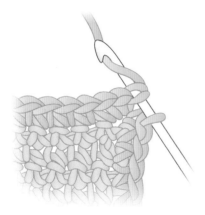 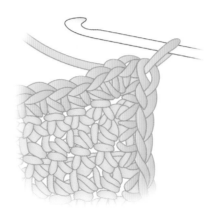

1 Work the single crochet edging all around. After completing the last stitch, insert the hook into the top of the first stitch and wrap the yarn over the hook.

2 Pull the yarn through both the stitch and loop on the hook to join the 2 stitches (1 loop on hook). Fasten off the yarn (see page 23).

Working a double crochet-group edging

This is a very effective and simple edging that works well with blankets. A double crochet group edging is created by making three double crochet in the same space each time all around the blanket. The instructions in the pattern will guide you where to place the double crochet and where to place the double crochet 2 stitches together (decrease). The double crochet 2 together decrease (see page 22) over the joins avoids the edging having too many stitches—which would make it curl—and creates a nice straight edge.

Abbreviations

[ ]	square parentheses indicate a repeat section
*	asterisk indicates beginning of repeated sequence
approx	approximately
beg	beginning
BLO	back loop only
ch	chain
ch sp	chain space
cm	centimeter(s)
cont	continu(e)(ing)
dc	double crochet
dc2tog	double crochet 2 stitches together
dtr	double treble
FLO	front loop only
g	gram(s)
hdc	half double crochet
hdcCL	half double crochet cluster
hdc2tog	half double crochet 2 stitches together
in	inch(es)
m	meter(s)
MC	main color
oz	ounce(s)
PC	popcorn
rep	repeat
RS	right side of work
sc	single crochet
sc2tog	single crochet 2 stitches together
sk	skip
sp(s)	space(s)
ss	slip stitch
st(s)	stitch(es)
tog	together
tr	treble
WS	wrong side of work
yd(s)	yard(s)
yoh	yarn over hook

Crochet stitch conversion chart

Crochet stitches are worked in the same way in both the USA and the UK, but the stitch names are not the same and identical names are used for different stitches.

Below is a list of the US terms used in this book, and the equivalent UK terms.

US TERM	UK TERM
single crochet (sc)	double crochet (dc)
half double crochet (hdc)	half treble (htr)
double crochet (dc)	treble (tr)
treble (tr)	double treble (dtr)
double treble (dtr)	triple treble (trtr)
gauge	tension
yarn over hook (yoh)	yarn round hook (yrh)

CHAPTER 1

FOR THE *Home*

Cotton Placemats

Skills needed:
- **Single crochet**
- **Working in rows**
- **Using a stitch marker**
- **Adding an edging**
- **Increasing**
- **Joining rounds with a slip stitch**

This is a great first project. You'll learn how to crochet in straight lines in a very basic single crochet stitch. Mix and match the colors and the edging to suit your color scheme. These are made using cotton yarn, so easy for washing!

YARN
Rowan Cotton Glacé, 100% cotton sportweight (lightweight DK) yarn, approx 125yd (115m) per 1¾oz (50g) ball:
For six placemats, 2 balls each of:
861 Rose (pink) (A)
849 Winsor (teal) (B)
749 Sky (pale blue) (C)
833 Ochre (yellow) (D)
725 Ecru (off-white) (E)
841 Garnet (dark purple) (F)

HOOK AND EQUIPMENT
US size E/4 (3.5mm) crochet hook
Yarn sewing needle

GAUGE
19 sts x 24 rows over a 4in (10cm) square, working single crochet using US size E/4 (3.5mm) hook and Rowan Cotton Glacé.

MEASUREMENTS
The finished placemat is 12 x 9¼in (30.5 x 23.5cm), including edging.

COLORWAYS
The six placemats are each worked in a different color, with a contrasting edging as follows:

Colorway 1: Placemat in A, edging in B
Colorway 2: Placemat in B, edging in A
Colorway 3: Placemat in C, edging in A
Colorway 4: Placemat in D, edging in C
Colorway 5: Placemat in E, edging in D
Colorway 6: Placemat in F, edging in E

ABBREVIATIONS
See page 27.

For the placemats
(make one each in A, B, C, D, E and F)
Foundation chain: Make 55ch.
Row 1 (RS): 1sc in 2nd ch from hook, 1sc in each ch to end. (54 sts)
Row 2: 1ch, 1sc in each sc to end. (Mark RS of work with a colored thread, so you will know which side to end on.)
Rep Row 2 until work measures 8½in (21.5cm), ending on a WS row. Cut yarn, but do not fasten off.
Edging: With the loop still on the hook after the last row and with RS facing, work a single crochet edging in rounds using a contrasting color.
Top of placemat: **Round 1 (RS):** 1ch to draw new color through loop on hook, 3sc in first sc (corner st of placemat). Cont along top edge, making 1sc in each sc along top of

placemat to last sc (next corner st), 3sc in corner st.
First side edge: *Measure halfway down first side edge and mark with a stitch or pin marker, 17sc evenly along side edge to marker, 17sc to next corner st.**
Bottom of placemat: 3sc in corner st, 52sc evenly along bottom edge to next corner (working 1sc in each ch along underside of foundation ch).
Second side edge: 3sc in corner st; rep from * to ** as for first side edge. Join round with a ss in first sc.
Do not turn the work, but cont with RS facing.
Round 2 (RS): 1ch, 1sc in first sc, 2sc in next sc (corner st), 1sc in each sc to next corner st (sc at center of 3-sc group), *2sc in center st of corner, 1sc in each sc to next corner st; rep from * to end, join with a ss in first sc.
Fasten off.

Making up and finishing
Using a yarn sewing needle, sew in all yarn ends. Block and press on the wrong side, covered with a damp cloth.

Tips

To stiffen your flags, try spraying with a little starch before hanging.

Making bunting out of your odds and ends of wool is ideal and a great way to use up spare wool left over from other projects.

If you use colors from different brands to get the yummy color scheme, just make sure the yarn is a similar weight.

Knickerbocker Glory Bunting

Bunting evokes all the atmosphere of spring and summer, whatever the weather and wherever you hang it. It's a lovely, happy way to brighten up a child's room, a garden, kitchen, hallway, or just about anywhere at all.

YARN

Debbie Bliss Rialto DK, 100% merino wool light worsted (DK) yarn, approx 115yd (105m) per 1¾oz (50g) ball:
  1 ball each of:
  19 Duck Egg (blue)
  65 Pale Pink (pale pink)
  64 Mauve (deep pink)
  85 Lilac
  59 Willow (light green)
  55 Coral

Debbie Bliss Falkland Aran, 100% wool worsted (aran) yarn, approx 197yd (180m) per 3½oz (100g) hank:
  1 hank of:
  07 Mustard (yellow)

HOOK AND EQUIPMENT

US size G/6 (4mm) crochet hook
Yarn sewing needle

GAUGE

Gauge is not critical on this project.

MEASUREMENTS

Each flag is approx 7in (18cm) across the top.

ABBREVIATIONS

See page 27.

For the flag

(make 6, or as many as required, in different colors with contrast edgings)
Make 26ch.
Row 1: 1sc in 2nd ch from hook, 1sc in each ch to end. (25 sts)
Row 2: 1ch, sc2tog, 1sc in each st to end.
Rep Row 2 until 2 sts remain, sc2tog.
Fasten off.

Top edging:
With RS facing, join in first contrast color into top right corner st, 3ch, make 24dc along top edge.
Fasten off.

Side edging:
With RS facing, join next contrast color in top left corner, 1ch, work 26sc along first side, 3sc in corner st, 26sc along other side ending with a ss into top of first dc.
Fasten off.
Sew in ends.

Making up and finishing

With contrasting color, make 70ch. With RS facing, join ch to first flag with ss in right-hand corner, 1ch, *1sc in between each dc across top of flag to end, join next flag with ss into top right-hand corner; rep from * to end for each flag, ss into last corner st of last flag. Make 70ch. Fasten off.

Using a yarn sewing needle at back of work, stitch to secure joins in between each flag using loose ends of yarn. Sew in ends well. Press each flag.

Round Stripy Pillow Cover

Skills needed:

- **Double crochet**
- **Joining rounds with a slip stitch**
- **Working into a ring**
- **Increasing**
- **Changing color**
- **Making a single crochet seam**

Crochet is perfect for making circles and this pillow cover is a project I've been teaching to all my beginner students for many years, because it is beautiful and easy to make. It uses simple double crochet stitch and the gorgeous range of Cashmerino Aran colors from Debbie Bliss.

YARN

Debbie Bliss Cashmerino Aran, 55% merino wool, 33% acrylic, 12% cashmere worsted (aran) yarn, approx 98yd (90m) per 1¾oz (50g) ball:

1 ball each of:

47 Aqua (light blue) (A)
84 Lilac (B)
603 Baby Pink (C)
09 Grey (D)
610 Ruby (red) (E)
76 Willow (green) (F)

HOOK AND EQUIPMENT

US size H/8 (5mm) crochet hook
16in (40cm) round pillow form

GAUGE

14 sts x 8 rows over a 4in (10cm) square, working double crochet using US size H/8 (5mm) hook and Debbie Bliss Cashmerino Aran.

MEASUREMENTS

The cover will fit a 16in (40cm) diameter pillow form.

ABBREVIATIONS

See page 27.

For the pillow

(make 2, front and back)
Using A, make 6ch, join with ss into first ch.
Round 1: 3ch (counts as first dc), 11dc into ring, join with a ss into top of first 3-ch.
Change to B.
Round 2: 3ch, 1dc into same st, 2dc into every st to end of round, join with a ss into top of first 3-ch. (24 sts)

Change to C.
Round 3: 3ch, 1dc into same st, *1dc into next st, 2dc into next 2 sts; rep from * to last 2 sts, 1dc into next st, 2dc into last st, join with a ss into top of first 3-ch. (40 sts)
Change to D.
Round 4: 3ch, 1dc into same st, *1dc into next 3 sts, 2dc into next st; rep from * to last 3 sts, 1dc into each of last 3 sts, join with a ss into top of first 3-ch. (50 sts)
Change to E.
Round 5: 3ch, 1dc into same st, *1dc into next 4 sts, 2dc into next st; rep from * to last 4 sts, 1dc into each of last 4 sts, join with ss into top of first 3-ch. (60 sts)
Change to F.
Round 6: 3ch, 1dc into same st, *1dc into next 5 sts, 2dc into next st; rep from * to last 5 sts, 1dc into each of last 5 sts, join with a ss into top of first 3-ch. (70 sts)
Change to A.
Round 7: 3ch, 1dc into same st, *1dc into next 6 sts, 2dc into next st; rep from * to last 6 sts, 1dc into each of last 6 sts, join with a ss

into top of first 3-ch. (80 sts)
Change to B.

Round 8: 3ch, 1dc into same st, *1dc into next 7 sts, 2dc into next st; rep from * to last 7 sts, 1dc into each of last 7 sts, join with a ss into top of first 3-ch. (90 sts)
Change to C.

Round 9: 3ch, 1dc into same st, *1dc into next 8 sts, 2dc into next st; rep from * to last 8 sts, 1dc into each of last 8 sts, join with a ss into top of first 3-ch. (100 sts)
Change to D.

Round 10: As Round 5. (120 sts)
Change to E.

Round 11: 3ch, 1dc into same st, *1dc into next 11 dc, 2dc in next st; rep from * to last 11 dc, 1dc in each of last 11 dc, join with a ss into top of first 3-ch. (130 sts)
Change to F.

Round 12: 3ch, 1dc into same st, *1dc into next 12 dc, 2dc in next st; rep from * to last 12 dc, 1dc into last 12 dc, join with a ss into top of first 3-ch.
Change to A.

Round 13: As Round 7.
Change to B.

Round 14: 3ch, 1dc into same st, *1dc into next 15 dc, 2dc in next st, rep from * to last 15 dc, 1dc in each of last 15 dc, join with a ss into top of first 3-ch.
Change to C.

Round 15: 3ch, 1dc into same st, *1dc into next 16 dc, 2dc in next st; rep from * to last 16 dc, 1dc in each of last 16 dc, join with a ss into top of first 3-ch.
Change to D.

Round 16: As Round 9.

Making up and finishing
Put pillow back and front WS facing. Insert hook into both pieces and, using A, make 1ch.

Make 1sc into each st, putting hook through both pieces to join edges together, leaving a big enough gap to push through pillow form. Cont in sc until seam is fully joined together.

Fasten off.

Sew in ends.

Jelly Pot Covers

These fun and original jelly pot covers are really quick and suitable for beginners. You can use any yarn—this pattern works with either double knit (light worsted) or aran (worsted) weight, although in aran the cover will come up slightly bigger.

Skills needed:

- **Single crochet**
- **Joining rounds with a slip stitch**
- **Double crochet**
- **Increasing**
- **Adding an edging**

YARN

Debbie Bliss Rialto DK, 100% merino wool light worsted (DK) yarn, approx 115yd (105m) per 1¾oz (50g) ball:

Colorway 1:
1 ball each of:
42 Pink (pale pink) (A)
02 Ecru (cream) (B)

Colorway 2:
1 ball each of:
85 Lilac (lavender) (A)
09 Apple (green) (B)

Colorway 3:
1 ball each of:
09 Apple (green) (A)
64 Mauve (pink) (B)

Colorway 4:
1 ball each of:
64 Mauve (pink) (A)
02 Ecru (cream) (B)

HOOK AND EQUIPMENT

US size G/6 (4mm) crochet hook
Approx 16in (40cm) each of:
Lime green bobble braiding
Pale blue ric-rac braiding
White ric-rac braiding
Yellow bobble braiding

GAUGE

Gauge is not critical on this project.

MEASUREMENTS

The standard cover is 6in (15cm) in diameter, the large cover is 7in (18cm) in diameter.

ABBREVIATIONS

See page 27.

For the covers

Using A, make 2ch, 6sc in second ch from hook, join with a ss.

Round 1: 3ch (counts as first dc), make 1dc into same st as 3-ch, 2dc into next and each st to end, join with a ss into top of first 3-ch. (12 sts)

Round 2: 3ch, make 1dc into same st as 3-ch, 2dc into next and each st to end, join with a ss into top of first 3-ch. (24 sts)

Round 3: 3ch, make 2dc into each of next 2 sts; *1dc into next st, 2dc in each of next 2 sts; rep from * to end, join with a ss into top of first 3-ch. (40 sts)

Round 4: 3ch, make 1dc into each of next 2 sts, *2dc into next st, 1dc in each of next 3 sts; rep from * to last st, 2dc, join with a ss into top of first 3-ch. (50 sts)

Tip

To make things easy to find, why not match the color of the cover or its trim to the contents of the pot?

Round 5: 3ch, make 1dc in next st, *2dc into next st, 1dc in each of next 2 sts; rep from * to last st, 1dc, join with a ss into top of first 3-ch. (66 sts)

Large size only:
Round 6: 3ch, make 1dc in each st, join with a ss into top of first 3ch. (66 sts)

Fasten off A and join B.
Round 7: With RS facing, skip 1 st, *5dc in next st, skip 1 st; rep from * to last st, ss to join.
Fasten off. (66 sts)

Making up and finishing
Block, press and sew in ends. You can tie the covers on with a length of ribbon, braid or bobble trim.

Pincushions

These little pincushions are just perfect for keeping pins and sewing needles safe. Choose colors from your stash as they use very little yarn. I use natural batting for the lining instead of fabric, because this makes it easier to push in pins or yarn sewing needles.

Skills needed:
- **Joining rounds with a slip stitch**
- **Working into a ring**
- **Single crochet**
- **Changing color**
- **Working a popcorn (see Note)**
- **Double crochet**
- **Working a sequence of stitches into one stitch**
- **Working into a chain space**
- **Half double crochet**
- **Adding an edging**

YARN

Colorway 1:
Debbie Bliss Rialto DK, 100% merino wool light worsted (DK) yarn, approx 115yd (105m) per 1¾oz (50g) ball:
 Small amounts each of:
 02 Ecru (cream) (A/B)
 42 Pink (pale pink) (C)
 19 Duck Egg (pale blue-green) (D/F)
 09 Apple (green) (E)

Colorway 2:
Debbie Bliss Falkland Aran, 100% wool worsted (aran) yarn, approx 197yd (180m) per 3½oz (100g) hank:
 Small amount of:
 07 Mustard (yellow) (A/C)

Debbie Bliss Rialto DK, 100% merino wool light worsted (DK) yarn, approx 115yd (105m) per 1¾oz (50g) ball:
 Small amounts each of:
 50 Deep Rose (deep pink) (B)
 19 Duck Egg (pale blue-green) (D)
 42 Pink (pale pink) (E)
 20 Teal (deep blue-green) (F)

Colorway 3:
Debbie Bliss Falkland Aran, 100% wool worsted (aran) yarn, approx 197yd (180m) per 3½oz (100g) hank:
 Small amount of:
 07 Mustard (yellow) (A)

Debbie Bliss Rialto DK, 100% merino wool light worsted (DK) yarn, approx 115yd (105m) per 1¾oz (50g) ball:
 Small amounts each of:
 42 Pink (pale pink) (B)
 50 Deep Rose (deep pink) (C)
 70 Pool (blue) (D/F)
 19 Duck Egg (pale blue-green) (E)

HOOK AND EQUIPMENT
US size G/6 (4mm) crochet hook
2 x 4¾in (12cm) squares of thin cotton fabric or natural batting and matching sewing thread
Small amount of toy stuffing

GAUGE
Front and back pieces (before edging is added) measure approx 2¾in (7cm) square, using US size G/6 (4mm) hook and Debbie Bliss Rialto DK.

MEASUREMENTS
Each pincushion is approx 4½in (11.5cm) square, including edging.

ABBREVIATIONS
See page 27.

NOTES
The pattern is for a two-color flower; for a one-color flower as on pincushion 1, do not fasten off on Round 1 but continue to use A for Round 2.
PC = popcorn stitch, worked with 5 double crochet (see page 22 for instructions, but work 5 double crochet instead of 4).

For the pincushion front
Using A, make 4ch, join with a ss in first ch to form a ring.
Round 1 (RS): 1ch, 8sc in ring, break off A (see Note), join B with a ss in first sc.

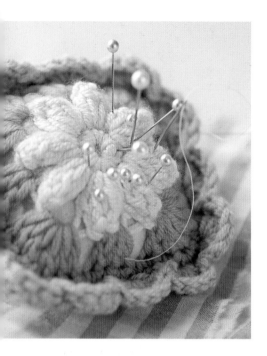

Cont in rounds with RS always facing.

Round 2: 3ch, 1PC in same sc as last ss, 2ch, [1PC in next sc, 2ch] 7 times, join with a ss in top of first PC. (8 petals)
Fasten off B.

Round 3: Join C with a ss in any 2-ch sp, 3ch (counts as first dc), [2dc, 1ch, 3dc] in same sp, 1ch, 3dc in next 2-ch sp, *1ch, [3dc, 1ch, 3dc] in next 2-ch sp, 1ch, 3dc in next ch sp; rep from * twice more, 1ch, join with a ss in top of first 3-ch.
Fasten off.

For the pincushion back

Using D, make 4ch, join with a ss to first ch to form a ring.

Round 1 (RS): 3ch, 2dc in ring, 2ch, [3dc in ring, 2ch] 3 times, join with a ss in top of first 3-ch.
Cont in rounds with RS always facing.

Round 2: 1ss in each of next 2 dc, 1ss in next 2-ch sp, 3ch, [2dc, 1ch, 3dc] in same sp, *1ch, [3dc, 1ch, 3dc] in next 2-ch sp; rep from * twice more, 1ch, join with a ss in top of first 3-ch.

Round 3: 1ss in each of next 2 dc, 1ss in next 1-ch sp, 2ch (counts as first hdc), [2hdc, 1ch, 3hdc] in same 1-ch sp, 1ch, 3hdc in next 1-ch sp, 1ch, *[3hdc, 1ch, 3hdc] in next 1-ch sp, 1ch, 3hdc in next 1-ch sp, 1ch; rep from * twice more, join with a ss in top of first 3-ch.
Fasten off. Sew in ends.

For the fabric pillow

With WS together, sew two fabric squares together, taking a ⅝in (1.5cm) seam allowance and leaving small opening in one side. Turn RS out, fill very firmly with toy stuffing and sew opening closed.

Making up and finishing

With front and back WS together, front facing upwards and working through both pieces, join E in any corner sp, 1ch, 2sc in same sp, *1sc in each st and ch sp to next corner, 2sc in corner; rep from * twice more, insert fabric pillow, 1sc in each st and ch sp to next corner (enclosing pillow), join with a ss in first sc.
Fasten off E.

Edging:
With front facing upward, join F with a ss in 2nd st to right of any 2-sc corner group, 5dc in 2nd sc of next 2-sc corner group, *skip 1 sc, 1ss in next sc, [skip 1sc, 5dc in next sc, skip 1 sc, 1ss in next sc] twice, 5dc in 2nd sc of next 2-sc corner group; rep from * twice, skip 1 sc, 1ss in next sc, [skip 1 sc, 5dc in next sc, skip 1 sc, 1ss in next sc] twice, working last ss in same place as first ss.

Fasten off.

Squares Baby Blanket

This blanket is made using traditional "granny" squares. They are the simplest squares to make, and this project is perfect for practicing double crochet, creating squares, making a wide edging, and using a double crochet decrease. A great project for those starting out, the blanket will be a much appreciated gift for a baby.

YARN

Debbie Bliss Baby Cashmerino, 55% merino wool, 33% acrylic, 12% cashmere sportweight (lightweight DK) yarn, approx 137yd (125m) per 1¾oz (50g) ball:

2 balls each of:
202 Light Blue (pale blue) (A)
034 Red

1 ball each of:
071 Pool (medium blue)
601 Baby Pink (pale pink)
101 Ecru (off-white)
078 Lipstick Pink (bright pink)
066 Amber (mustard yellow)
002 Apple (light green)
010 Lilac

HOOK AND EQUIPMENT

US size E/4 (3.5mm) crochet hook
Yarn sewing needle

GAUGE

Each square measures 2½ x 2½in (6.5 x 6.5cm) using a US size E/4 (3.5mm) hook and Debbie Bliss Baby Cashmerino.

MEASUREMENTS

The finished blanket measures 28¾ x 33¾in (74.5 x 87.5cm), including edging, which is ⅝in (1.5cm) wide.

ABBREVIATIONS

See page 27.

For the squares

(make 143, in assorted colors)

Foundation ring: Make 4ch and join with a ss in first ch to form a ring.

Round 1 (RS): 3ch (counts as first dc), 2dc in ring, 2ch, [3dc in ring, 2ch] 3 times, join with a ss in top of first 3-ch. (four 3-dc groups) Cont in rounds with RS always facing you.

Round 2: 1ss in each of next 2dc, 1ss in next 2-ch sp, 3ch (counts as first dc), [2dc, 2ch, 3dc] in same ch sp (corner), *[3dc, 2ch, 3dc] in next 2-ch sp; rep from * twice more, join with a ss in top of first 3-ch.

Round 3: 1ss in each of next 2dc, 1ss in next 2-ch sp, 3ch (counts as first dc), [2dc, 2ch, 3dc] in same 2-ch sp (corner), 3dc in next sp between next two 3-dc groups, *[3dc, 2ch, 3dc] in next 2-ch sp (corner), 3dc in next sp between next two 3-dc groups; rep from * twice more, join with a ss in top of first 3-ch.
Fasten off.

Making up and finishing

Using a yarn sewing needle, sew in any remaining yarn ends. Block and press each square on the WS.

With RS facing up, place the squares on a flat surface and arrange them in 13 horizontal rows (length) of 11 squares each (width). Make sure the colored squares are evenly spaced.

With RS together and using A (pale blue) and a yarn sewing needle, join the squares in 13 rows using whip stitch. Then join the rows together.

Block and lightly press the seams on the WS of the blanket.

For the double crochet-group edging

Round 1 (RS): With RS facing and using A (pale blue), join yarn with a ss in a 2-ch sp at one corner of the blanket, 3ch (counts as first dc), [2dc, 2ch, 3dc] in same corner sp, 3dc in each of next 2 sps between 3-dc groups, *1dc in last sp of this square (corner of square), dc2tog over same corner sp and first corner sp of next square, 1dc in same corner sp, 3dc in each of next 2 sps between 3-dc groups*; rep from * to * to next blanket corner, **[3dc, 2ch, 3dc] in corner 2-ch sp, rep from * to * to next blanket corner; rep from ** to end, join with a ss in top of first 3-ch.

Round 2: 1ss in each of next 2dc, 1ss in corner 2-ch sp, 3ch (counts as 1dc), [2dc, 2ch, 3dc] in same corner sp, 3dc in next and each sp between dc groups to next corner (skip each dc2tog in previous round, do not make double crochet in center of these dc2tog), *[3dc, 2ch, 3dc] in corner 2-ch sp, 3dc in next and each sp between dc groups to next corner; rep from * to end, join with a ss in first 3-ch. Fasten off.

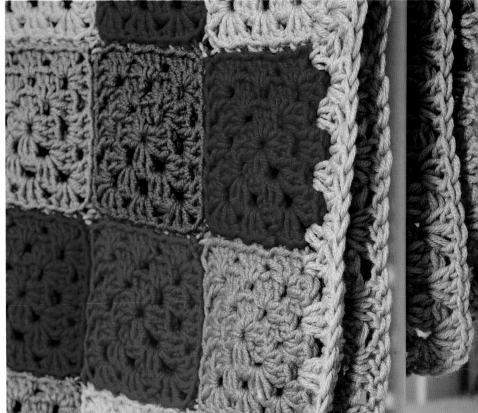

Mug Warmers

This is a very simple little project and a fun way to liven up your breakfast table in the morning.

Skills needed:
- **Working in rows**
- **Half double crochet**
- **Making a chain button loop**
- **Adding an edging**

YARN

Colorway 1:
Rooster Almerino Aran, 50% baby alpaca, 50% merino wool worsted (aran) yarn, approx 103yd (94m) per 1¾oz (50g) ball:
  1 ball of 303 Strawberry Cream

Colorway 2:
Rooster Almerino Aran, 50% baby alpaca, 50% merino wool worsted (aran) yarn, approx 103yd (94m) per 1¾oz (50g) ball:
  1 ball of 309 Ocean (blue-green)

HOOK AND EQUIPMENT
US size 7 (4.5mm) crochet hook
Yarn sewing needle
1 small button

GAUGE
Gauge is not critical on this project.

MEASUREMENTS
The warmer will fit a mug 3in (7.5cm) in diameter across the top.

ABBREVIATIONS
See page 27.

For the mug warmers
Make 32ch.
Row 1: 1hdc in third ch from hook, 1hdc in each ch to end. (30 sts)
Row 2: 2ch, 1hdc in each st to end.
Row 3: 2ch, 2hdc in first st, 1hdc in each st to last st, 2hdc. (32 sts)
Row 4: 2ch, 2hdc in first st, 1hdc in each st to last st, 2hdc. (34 sts)
Row 5: 2ch, 1hdc in each st.
Row 6: 2ch, 1hdc in each st. At end of row, do not turn, make 8ch, ss approx ½in (1cm) down the side of work. Do not fasten off.

Edging:
Make 4sc evenly along first side edge, 3sc in corner st, 30sc along bottom edge, 3sc in corner st, 5sc along second side edge, 3sc in corner st, 1sc in each st across top, 1sc into each ch around button fastener, ss into first sc.
Fasten off.

Making up and finishing
Sew side seam up to base of handle. Sew on button to correspond with button fastener. Place mug inside cover and fasten.

cafetière cozy

Skills needed:
- **Working in rows**
- **Single crochet**
- **Changing color**
- **Making a buttonhole**

A fun and easy project to keep the coffee in your French press toastie and warm. The colors are changed at random as you work, for a multicolor effect.

YARN

Debbie Bliss Falkland Aran, 100% wool worsted (aran) yarn, approx 197yd (180m) per 3½oz (100g) hank:

1 hank each of:
07 Mustard (yellow)
15 Ruby (red)
16 Blossom (bright pink)
10 Teal (blue-green)
11 Duck Egg (pale blue)
13 Purple

Debbie Bliss Cashmerino Aran, 55% merino wool, 33% acrylic, 12% cashmere worsted (aran) yarn, approx 98yd (90m) per 1¾oz (50g) ball:

1 ball of:
603 Baby Pink (pale pink)

HOOK AND EQUIPMENT

US size H/8 (5mm) crochet hook
Yarn sewing needle
1 small button

GAUGE

16 sts x 20 rows over a 4in (10cm) square, working single crochet using US size H/8 (5mm) hook and Debbie Bliss Falkland Aran.

MEASUREMENTS

The cozy will fit a medium-size 4–6 cup cafetière, approx 12in (31cm) in circumference.

ABBREVIATIONS

See page 27.

For the cozy

Using any color, make 46ch.
Row 1: 1sc into next ch from hook, 1sc into each ch to end, turn. (45 sts)

Row 2: 1ch, 1sc into each st to end. Rep Row 2, changing colors randomly every 2, 3, or 4 rows, until work measures 6¼in 16cm), or to just above handle of cafetière. Do not fasten off.

Make buttonhole and button tab:
Make 5ch, 1sc into next ch from hook, 1sc into each st to end, turn.
Next row: 1sc into each st to last 4 sts, make 2ch, skip 2 sts, 1sc into each of next 2 sts.
Next row: 1ch, 1sc into each of next 2 sts, 2sc into next ch sp, 1sc into each st to end.
Next row: 1sc into each st to end. Do not fasten off.
Work sc around button tab by making 2sc around side, 1sc in each of the sts underneath to end. Make ss into straight edge.
Fasten off.

Making up and finishing

With WS facing, sew a seam 1in (2.5cm) up from the bottom, leaving remainder open. Turn RS out. Sew a button to correspond with buttonhole. Sew in ends.

Egg Cozies

Skills needed:
- **Working in rounds**
- **Single crochet**
- **Single crochet 2 stitches together decrease**
- **Joining rounds with a slip stitch**
- **Working into a ring**
- **Double crochet**

Keep your breakfast eggs warm with these really cute cozies. They are very easy to make once you get the idea of crocheting in the spiral. Use a stitch marker to keep track of the beginning of each round—a scrap of a contrasting strand of yarn threaded through the stitch will do.

YARN

Egg cozies:

Debbie Bliss Rialto DK, 100% merino wool light worsted (DK) yarn, approx 115yd (105m) per 1¾oz (50g) ball:

Small amounts of:
02 Ecru (cream) (A)
85 Lilac (pale grey-lilac) (B)
55 Coral (orange) (C)
64 Mauve (bright pink) (D)
44 Aqua (pale turquoise) (E)
57 Banana (pale yellow) (F)

Flowers:

Debbie Bliss Baby Cashmerino, 55% wool, 33% acrylic, 12% cashmere sportweight (lightweight DK) yarn, approx 137yd (125m) per 1¾oz (50g) ball:

Scraps of:
10 Lilac (lavender) (G)
06 Candy Pink (pink) (H)
65 Clotted Cream (cream) (J)
93 Clematis (deep pink) (K)
01 Primrose (yellow) (L)
89 Sapphire (aqua) (M)

HOOK AND EQUIPMENT

US size B/1 (2mm) and US size E/4 (3.5mm) crochet hooks

GAUGE

17 sts x 19 rows over a 4in (10cm) square, working single crochet using US size E/4 (3.5mm) hook and Debbie Bliss Rialto DK.

MEASUREMENTS

Each cozy is approx 1½in (4cm) in diameter.

ABBREVIATIONS

See page 27.

For the cozy

(make 1 each in A, B, C, D, E and F)
Using US size E/4 (3.5mm) hook, make 2ch, 6sc into 2nd ch from hook.

Round 1 (RS): 2sc in each sc to end. (12 sts)
Cont in rounds with RS always facing.

Round 2: Rep Round 1. (24 sts)

Rounds 3–7: 1sc in each sc to end.

Round 8: *1sc in next sc, sc2tog over next 2 sc; rep from * to end. (16 sts)

Round 9: 1sc in each sc, join with a ss in first sc of round.
Fasten off.

For the flowers

(make 1 each in G, H, J, K, L and M)
Using US size B/1 (2mm) hook, 4ch, join with a ss in first ch to form a ring.

Round 1 (RS): 1ch, 8sc in ring, join with a ss in first sc.
Cont with RS facing.
Round 2: *3ch, 1dc in same place as last ss, 1dc in next st, 3ch, 1ss in same place as last dc, 1ss in next st; rep from * to end, omitting last ss of last rep. (4 petals)
Fasten off.

Making up and finishing

Sew in ends on the WS and turn cozy RS out.
Using contrasting color (G, H, J, K, L or M), make 5 or 6 bullion or French knots in center of each flower. Sew one flower on top of each cozy.

Springtime Throw

This is a delightful project and the squares are very easy and perfect for a beginner. It's the colors of the Rooster yarn that make this so special—but it also works well using scraps of yarn.

Skills needed:
- Working into a ring
- Single crochet
- Double crochet
- Changing color
- Working into a chain space
- Making a single crochet seam
- Adding an edging

YARN

Rooster Almerino DK, 50% baby alpaca, 50% merino wool light worsted (DK) yarn, approx 124yd (112.5m) per 1¾oz (50g) ball:

21 balls of 201 Cornish (cream) (MC)

5 balls each of:
209 Smoothie (deep pink)
207 Gooseberry (green)
203 Strawberry Cream (light pink)
205 Glace (pale blue)
204 Grape (purple)
210 Custard (yellow)

HOOK AND EQUIPMENT

US size G/6 (4mm) crochet hook
Yarn sewing needle

GAUGE

Gauge is not critical on this project.

MEASUREMENTS

The finished throw is approx 64 x 88in (162 x 223cm).

ABBREVIATIONS

See page 27.

COLORWAYS

Make 432 squares in total: 14 each of 30 different color combinations (420 squares), plus another 12 random colorways. On every square, Round 2 is made using MC.

For the square

Using first color, make a loop, then make 4ch. Join with ss into first ch to form a ring.

Round 1: 3ch, 2dc into ring, 2ch, 3dc into ring, 2ch, *3dc into ring, 2ch; rep from * once more.
Ss into top of first 3-ch.
Fasten off.
Place hook through a ch sp and join in MC.

Round 2: 3ch, 2dc, 3ch, 3dc into same ch sp (first corner), 2ch, *3dc, 3ch, 3dc into next ch sp, 2ch; rep from * twice more.
Ss into top of first 3-ch.
Fasten off.
Put hook into top of fastened-off stitch, join in third color, make 1ch.

Round 3: 1sc into top of next 2 sts, 3sc into next ch sp, 1sc into top of next 3 sts, 2sc into next ch sp, *1sc into top of next 3 sts, 3sc into next ch sp, 1sc into top of next 3 sts, 2sc into next ch sp; rep from * twice more.

Ss into top of first ch.
Fasten off.
Sew in ends neatly and securely after making each square.

Making up and finishing

Lay out the squares with 18 squares across (width) by 24 squares down (length) in a random order. Using MC and with WS together, join squares first in horizontal rows and then in vertical rows, using a sc seam. When all squares are joined, work one row of sc edging all the way around blanket. When turning corners, make 2sc, 1ch, 2sc into each corner stitch.

Fasten off.
Sew in ends.

Tip

This is a large blanket and takes up a lot of balls of yarn. It's made up from lots of small squares, so it's very easy to adjust the sizing by making fewer or more squares; just remember to adjust the yarn quantities.

TO *Wear*

Chunky Patchwork Scarf

An outrageously long, chunky, and bright scarf for instant style!

YARN

Debbie Bliss Cashmerino Aran, 55% merino wool, 33% acrylic, 12% cashmere worsted (aran) yarn, approx 98yd (90m) per 1¾oz (50g) ball:
  4 balls of 300 Black (MC)

Rooster Almerino Aran, 50% baby alpaca, 50% merino wool worsted (aran) yarn, approx 103yd (94m) per 1¾oz (50g) ball:
  2 balls of 301 Cornish (cream)
  1 ball each of:
  310 Rooster (red)
  302 Sugared Almond (pale blue)
  309 Ocean (blue-green)
  318 Coral (orange)
  307 Brighton Rock (deep pink)
  305 Custard (yellow)
  315 Shimmer (pale grey)
  306 Gooseberry (green)
  319 Lilac Sky (pale grey-lilac)
  311 Deep Sea (deep blue)

HOOK AND EQUIPMENT

US size H/8 (5mm) crochet hook
Yarn sewing needle

GAUGE

Each square measures 6in (15cm), using US size H/8 (5mm) hook and Debbie Bliss Cashmerino Aran.

MEASUREMENTS

The finished scarf is 118in (300cm) long and 12in (30cm) wide.

ABBREVIATIONS

See page 27.

COLORWAYS

Use four colors at random in Rounds 1, 2, 3, and 4, occasionally using same color for Rounds 2 and 4, 1, and 4, or 2, and 3. Always use MC in Round 5.

For the square

(make 40)
Using first color, make 4ch, join with ss to form a ring.
Round 1: 3ch, 2dc in ring, 2ch, *[3dc, 2ch] in ring; rep from * twice more (4-dc groups), join with ss in top of first 3-ch.
Fasten off first color.
With RS facing, join 2nd color in any 2-ch sp.
Round 2: 3ch, [2dc, 2ch, 3dc] in same ch sp, *1ch, [3dc, 2ch, 3dc] in next ch sp; rep from * twice more, 1ch, join with ss in top of first 3-ch.
Fasten off 2nd color.
With RS facing, join 3rd color in next 2-ch sp (corner).

Round 3: 3ch, [2dc, 2ch, 3dc] in same ch sp, *1ch, 3dc in next ch sp, 1ch, [3dc, 2ch, 3dc] in next ch sp (corner); rep from * twice more, 1ch, 3dc in next ch sp, 1ch, join with ss in top of first 3-ch.
Fasten off 3rd color.
With RS facing, join 4th color in next 2-ch sp (corner).
Round 4: 3ch, [2dc, 2ch, 3dc] in same ch sp, *[1ch, 3dc in next ch sp] twice, 1ch, [3dc, 2ch, 3dc] in next ch sp (corner); rep from * twice more, [1ch, 3dc in next ch sp] twice, 1ch, join with ss in top of first 3-ch.
Fasten off 4th color.
With RS facing, join MC in next 2-ch sp (corner).
Round 5: 3ch, [2dc, 2ch, 3dc] in same ch sp (corner), *[1ch, 3dc in next ch sp] 3 times in each of next 3 ch sps, 1ch, [3dc, 2ch, 3dc] in next ch sp (corner); rep from * twice more, [1ch, 3dc in next ch sp] 3 times, 1ch, join with ss in top of first 3-ch.
Fasten off, sew in ends.

Making up and finishing

Join squares together in 20 rows of 2 with a sc seam. Sew in ends.

Beanie Hat

A must-have basic beanie hat, crocheted in a supersoft cashmere and merino wool mix that looks and feels great.

Skills needed:

- **Joining rounds with a slip stitch**
- **Working in rounds**
- **Single crochet**
- **Half double crochet**
- **Half double crochet 2 stitches together decrease**

YARN

Debbie Bliss Baby Cashmerino, 55% wool, 33% acrylic, 12% cashmere sportweight (lightweight DK) yarn, approx 137yd (125m) per 1¾oz (50g) ball:

  2 balls of 203 Teal (blue)

HOOK AND EQUIPMENT

US size E/4 (3.5mm) crochet hook
Yarn sewing needle

GAUGE

18 sts x 14 rows over a 4in (10cm) square, working half double crochet using US size E/4 (3.5mm) hook and Debbie Bliss Baby Cashmerino.

MEASUREMENTS

The finished hat measures 19¾in (50cm) in circumference and 7in (18cm) deep.

ABBREVIATIONS

See page 27.

For the hat

Make 90ch, join with ss in first ch to form a ring.

Round 1: 1ch, skip st at base of ch, 1sc in each ch, join with ss in first ch. (90 sts)
Round 2: 1ch, skip st at base of ch, 1sc in each st, join with ss in first ch.
Rounds 3–12: Rep Round 2.
Round 13: 2ch, skip st at base of ch, 1hdc in each st to end, join with ss in top of first 2-ch.
Rounds 14–24: Rep Round 13.
Round 25: 2ch, skip st at base of ch, *1hdc in each of next 9 sts, hdc2tog; rep from * to last st, 1hdc in last st, join with ss in top of first 2-ch. (82 sts)
Round 26: Rep Round 13.
Round 27: 2ch, skip st at base of ch, 1hdc in each of next 8 sts, hdc2tog; rep from * to last st, 1hdc in last st, join with ss in top of first 2-ch. (74 sts)
Round 28: Rep Round 13.
Round 29: 2ch, skip st at base of ch, *1hdc in each of next 7 sts, hdc2tog; rep from * to last st, 1hdc in last st, join with ss in top of first 2-ch. (66 sts)

Round 30: 2ch, skip st at base of ch, *1hdc in each of next 6 sts, hdc2tog; rep from * to last st, 1hdc in last st, join with ss in top of first 2-ch. (58 sts)
Round 31: 2ch, skip st at base of ch, *1hdc in each of next 5 sts, hdc2tog; rep from * to last st, 1hdc in last st, join with ss in top of first 2-ch. (50 sts)
Round 32: 2ch, skip st at base of ch, *1hdc in each of next 4 sts, hdc2tog; rep from * to last st, 1hdc in last st, join with ss in top of first 2-ch. (42 sts)
Round 33: 2ch, skip st at base of ch, *1hdc in each of next 3 sts, hdc2tog; rep from * to last st, 1hdc in last st, join with ss in top of first 2-ch. (34 sts)
Fasten off, leaving an approx 8in (20cm) tail.

Making up and finishing

Working on WS of hat and using yarn needle, thread tail and insert needle through top of each st at top of hat, pull tightly to close hole and fasten off. Allow brim to roll up on RS.

Brimmed Baby Hat

A very pretty and cute hat for a toddler. This is made in a fine wool/silk yarn, which is very soft and easy to wear. Perfect both for keeping the sun off baby's head or keeping nice and warm in the winter.

YARN

Fyberspates Scrumptious 4ply, 55% merino wool, 45% silk fingering (4ply) yarn, approx 399yd (365m) per 3½oz (100g) hank:

  1 x hank of 304 Water (grey) (A)

Rooster Almerino DK, 50% baby alpaca, 50% merino wool light worsted (DK) yarn, approx 124yd (112.5m) per 1¾oz (50g) ball:

  Small amount of 211 Brighton Rock (bright pink) (B)

HOOK AND EQUIPMENT

US size C/2 (3mm) and US size G/6 (4mm) crochet hooks
Yarn sewing needle

GAUGE

Gauge is not critical on this project, but try to achieve a fairly firm fabric.

MEASUREMENTS

The finished hat is approx 17–18in (42.5–45cm) in circumference, to fit age 12–36 months.

For the hat

Using US size C/2 (3mm) hook and yarn A, make 5ch. Join with ss in first ch to make a ring.

Round 1: 12dc in ring.
Mark first sc of each round with a st marker.

Round 2: *1sc in next dc, 2sc in next dc; rep from * to end. (18 sts)

Round 3: *1sc in each of next 2 sts, 2sc in next st; rep from * to end. (24 sts)

Round 4: *1sc in each of next 3 sts, 2sc in next st; rep from * to end. (30 sts)

Round 5: *1sc in each of next 4 sts, 2sc in next st; rep from * to end. (36 sts)

Round 6: *1sc in each of next 5 sts, 2sc in next st; rep from * to end. (42 sts)

Round 7: *1sc in each of next 6 sts, 2sc in next st; rep from * to end. (48 sts)

Round 8: *1sc in each of next 7 sts, 2sc in next st; rep from * to end. (54 sts)

Round 9: *1sc in each of next 8 sts, 2sc in next st; rep from * to end. (60 sts)

Round 10: *1sc in each of next 9 sts, 2sc in next st; rep from * to end. (66 sts)

Round 11: *1sc in each of next 10 sts, 2sc in next st; rep from * to end. (72 sts)

Round 12: *1sc in each of next 11 sts, 2sc in next st; rep from * to end. (78 sts)

Round 13: *1sc in each of next 12 sts, 2sc in next st; rep from * to end. (84 sts)

Round 14: *1sc in each of next 13 sts, 2sc in next st; rep from * to end. (90 sts)

Round 15: *1sc in each of next 14 sts, 2sc in next st; rep from * to end. (96 sts)

Round 16: *1sc in each of next 15 sts, 2sc in next st; rep from * to end. (102 sts)

Round 17: *1sc in each of next 16 sts, 2sc in next st; rep from * to end. (108 sts)

Round 18: *1sc in each of next 17 sts, 2sc in next st; rep from * to end. (114 sts)

Round 19: 1sc in each st. (114 sts) Mark first sc2tog of Rounds 20–28 with a st marker.

Round 20: 1ch (counts as st), *sc2tog, 1ch; rep from * to end. (115 sts)

Round 21: *sc2tog (by drawing yarn through 1ch-sp at either side of sc2tog below), 1ch; rep from * to end. (114 sts)

Rounds 22–28: Rep Round 21. (114 sts)

Rounds 29–31: 1sc in each st. (114 sts)

Make brim:

Round 32: *1sc in each of next 5 sts, 2sc in next st; rep from * to end. (133 sts)

Rounds 33–36: 1sc in each st. (133 sts)

Round 37: *1sc in each of next 6 sts, 2sc in next st; rep from * to end. (152 sts)

Rounds 38–40: 1sc in each st. (152 sts)

Round 41: *1sc in each of next 7 sts, 2sc in next st; rep from * to end. (171 sts)

Rounds 42–43: 1sc in each st. (171 sts)
Fasten off.

Flowers

(make 3)

Using A and US size G/6 (4mm) hook, make 6ch, join with ss into first ch to make a ring.
Make 16sc into ring, join with ss. Fasten off.
Join B into fastened-off st.
*3ch, 1dc into next 2 sts, 3ch, ss into next st; rep from * 4 times (5 petals).
Fasten off.

Making up and finishing

Sew in ends on hat.

Using a yarn sewing needle, weave around the center hole of flower to close and tighten; sew in ends. Position flowers as required and stitch to hat.

Ear Flap Hat

Look stylish, while keeping your ears warm at the same time, with this fashionable hat.

Skills needed:

- Half double crochet
- Working in rounds
- Increasing
- Using a stitch marker
- Half double crochet 2 stitches together decrease
- Adding an edging
- Joining rounds with a slip stitch
- Working into a ring
- Treble

YARN

Hat:
Rooster Almerino Aran, 50% baby alpaca, 50% merino wool worsted (aran) yarn, approx 103yd (94m) per 1¾oz (50g) ball:
  3 balls of 320 Silver (A)
  1 ball of 318 Coral (orange) (B)

Flowers:
Rooster Almerino DK, 50% baby alpaca, 50% merino wool light worsted (DK) yarn, approx 124yd (112.5m) per 1¾oz (50g) ball:
  Small amount each of:
  210 Custard (yellow) (C)
  201 Cornish (cream) (D)

HOOK AND EQUIPMENT

US size C/2 (3mm), US size H/8 (5mm) and US size J/10 (6mm) crochet hooks
Yarn sewing needle

GAUGE

11 sts x 9 rows over a 4in (10cm) square, working half double crochet using US size J/10 (6mm) hook and two strands of Rooster Almerino Aran.

MEASUREMENTS

The small size is 20in (50cm) in circumference, the large size is 21¾in (54.5cm) in circumference.

ABBREVIATIONS

See page 27.

NOTES

The hat is made by starting from the top and working down in a spiral. Mark the beginning and end of each round by inserting a stitch marker in the loop on the hook at the beginning of each round.

Use yarn double by using two balls of yarn, with one strand from each held together.

For the hat

Use A double, and US size J/10 (6mm) hook.

Round 1 (RS): 3ch (counts as first hdc), 9hdc in 3rd ch from hook. (10 sts) Cont in rounds with RS always facing.

Round 2: 2hdc in top of 2ch at beg of Round 1, 2hdc in each of next 9 hdc. (20 sts)

Round 3: *1hdc in next st, 2hdc in next st; rep from * to end. (30 sts)

Round 4: *1hdc in each of next 2 sts, 2hdc in next st; rep from * to end. (40 sts)

Round 5: *1hdc in each of next 3 sts, 2hdc in next st; rep from * to end. (50 sts)

Small size only:

Round 6: *1hdc in each of next 9 sts, 2hdc in next st; rep from * to end. (55 sts)

Round 7: *1hdc in each st to end.
Rounds 8–15: Rep Round 7.

Large size only:

Round 6: *1hdc in each of next 4 sts, 2hdc in next st; rep from * to end. (60 sts)

Round 7: *1hdc in each st to end.
Rounds 8–17: Rep Round 7.

Both sizes:

Fasten off one strand only, do not break off second strand. Cont working with one strand of yarn only and using US size H/8 (5mm) hook.

First ear flap:

Put st marker in loop on hook.
*With RS facing, make 1hdc in each of next 12 sts, turn.

Next row: 2ch, hdc2tog over first two sts, 1hdc in next 8 sts, hdc2tog. (10 sts)
Next row: 2ch, hdc2tog, 1hdc in next 6 sts, hdc2tog. (8 sts)
Next row: 2ch, hdc2tog, 1hdc in next 4 sts, hdc2tog. (6 sts)
Next row: 2ch, hdc2tog, 1hdc in next 2 sts, hdc2tog. (4 sts)
Fasten off.

Second ear flap:

With RS facing and using US size H/8 (5mm) hook and one strand of A only, fold hat flat and on opposite side to first flap, join yarn with a ss in st to correspond with last st of first row (of first flap), place marker in loop, 1ch; rep from * of First Ear Flap.

Edging:

Round 1 (RS): Using US size H/8 (5mm) hook and one strand of B, join yarn with a ss in first st of first flap, 1ch, 1sc in same place as ss, work a total of 20 sc evenly around flap (working 2sc in corners), 1sc in each st to next flap, work 20sc evenly around flap (working 2sc in corners), 1sc in each st to end, join with a ss in first sc.
Fasten off.

For the flowers

(make 2)

Using US size C/2 (3mm) hook and C, make 4ch, join with a ss in first ch to form a ring.

Round 1 (RS): 1ch, 18sc in ring, break off C, join D with a ss in first sc. Cont with RS facing.

Round 2: [4ch, 1tr in next st, 4ch, 1ss in next st] 9 times, working last ss at base of first 4ch. (9 petals)
Fasten off.

Making up and finishing

Sew in ends on hat.

Close hole in center of flowers by sewing around center with tail of yarn C. Sew in ends to tidy up flower. Block, starch and press flowers. Arrange flowers on side at front of hat and sew in place.

Fingerless Gloves

These are lovely and simple and so desirable I have a line of people waiting for a pair! They are one size and made to fit an average-sized woman, but if you want to make them bigger, try using smaller size hooks or a thinner wool such as light worsted (DK).

YARN

Rooster Almerino Aran, 50% baby alpaca, 50% merino wool worsted (aran) yarn, approx 103yd (94m) per 1¾oz (50g) ball:
  2 balls of 311 Deep Sea (dark blue) (A)

Debbie Bliss Angel, 76% super kid mohair, 24% silk laceweight yarn, approx 219yd (200m) per ⅞oz (25g) ball:
  Small amount of 31 Raspberry (deep pink) (B)

Rooster Delightful Lace, 80% baby alpaca, 20% silk laceweight yarn, approx 874yd (800m) per 3½oz (100g) hank:
  Scrap of 601 Cusco (off-white) (C)

HOOK AND EQUIPMENT

US size B/1 (2mm), US size E/4 (3.5mm) and US size 7 (4.5mm) crochet hooks
Yarn sewing needle

GAUGE

16 sts x 9 rows over a 4in (10cm) square, working double crochet using US size 7 (4.5mm) hook and Rooster Almerino Aran.

MEASUREMENTS

To fit an average-sized woman's hand.

ABBREVIATIONS

See page 27.

NOTES

This pattern is made in the round, place a stitch marker in the beginning loop of each round, starting at Round 1.

There are also two different stitch markers for the thumb position on increasing rounds, use a contrasting color for these markers.

For the glove

(make 1 pair)
Starting at wrist end.
Using A and US size 7 (4.5mm) hook, make 32ch, join with a ss in first ch to form a ring. Place

st marker (count marked st as last st) and change to US size E/4 (3.5mm) hook.
Round 1 (RS): 1dc in each ch to end. (32 sts)
Cont in rounds with RS always facing.

Round 2: Dc2tog, 1dc in each of next 14 sts, dc2tog, 1dc in each st to end. (30 sts)

Round 3: 1dc in each st to end. (30 sts)

Round 4: 1dc in each st to end.

Round 5: 1dc in each st to end.

Round 6: 1dc in each st to end.

Round 7: 1dc in each of next 12 sts, 2dc in next st (place thumb marker in first of these 2dc), 1dc in next st, 2dc in next st (place second thumb marker in last of these 2dc), 1dc in each st to end. (32 sts)

Round 8: 1dc in each st to end. (32 sts)

Round 9: 1dc in each st to first thumb marker, 2dc in next st—the one with thumb marker—(replace thumb marker in first of these 2dc), 1dc in each st to next thumb marker, 2dc in next st—the one with thumb marker—(replace second thumb marker in last of these 2dc), 1dc in each st to end of round. (34 sts)

Round 10: 1dc in each st to first thumb marker, 2dc in next st (replace thumb marker in first of these 2dc), 1dc in each st to next thumb marker, 2dc in next st (replace second thumb marker in last of these 2dc), 1dc in each st to end. (36 sts)

Round 11: 1dc in each st to end. (36 sts)

Round 12: 1dc in each st to first thumb marker, 2dc in next st (replace thumb marker in first of these 2dc), 1dc in each st to next thumb marker, 2dc in next st (replace second thumb marker in last of these 2dc), 1dc in each st to end. (38 sts)

Round 13: 1dc in each st to end. (38 sts)

Round 14: 1dc in each st to first thumb marker, 2dc in next st (replace thumb marker in first of these 2dc), 1dc in each st to next thumb marker, 2dc in next st (replace second thumb marker in last of these 2dc), 1dc in each st to end. (40 sts)

Round 15: 1dc in each st to first thumb marker, skip 13 sts, 1dc in next st, 1dc in each st to end. (28 sts)

Remove thumb st markers only. Do not remove st marker to indicate beg of round.

Round 16: 1dc in each st to end. (27 sts)

Round 17: 1dc in each st to end. (27 sts)

Round 18: 1hdc in each st to last 2 sts, hdc2tog. (26 sts)

Round 19: 1sc in each st to last 2 sts, sc2tog. (25 sts)

Round 20: 1sc in each st to end, join with a ss in last st. (25 sts)

Fasten off.

Thumbhole:
With RS facing and using US size E/4 (3.5mm) hook, join A with a ss in first st of 13 sts skipped for thumbhole in Round 15.

Round 1 (RS): 1ch, 1 sc in same place as last ss (place st marker), 1sc in each of next 12 sts around thumbhole. (13 sts)

Cont to work thumb in rounds with RS always facing.

Round 2: 1sc in first sc, 1sc in each each st to last 2 sts, sc2tog. (12 sts)

Round 3: 1sc in each st to end. (12 sts)

Round 4: 1sc in each st to last st, 1ss in last st.

Fasten off.

Edging:
With RS facing and using US size E/4 (3.5mm) hook, join A with a ss in underside of first chain at wrist end of glove.

Round 1 (RS): 1sc in each ch to end, join with a ss in first sc. (32 sts)

Cont with RS facing.

Round 2: 1ch, 1sc in same place as last ss, skip 1 st, 5dc in next st, skip 1 st, *1sc in next st, skip 1 st, 5dc in next st, skip 1 st; rep from * to end, join with a ss in first sc.

Fasten off.

For the flowers
(make 28)

Using B and US size B/1 (2mm) hook, make 4ch, join with a ss in first ch to form a ring.

Round 1 (RS): [3ch, 1ss in ring] 5 times, join with a ss in base of first 3-ch.

Fasten off.

Sew around hole in center to close.

Making up and finishing
Sew in ends.

Turn glove inside out and hand sew gap at base of thumbhole to close it.

Using C, make a French knot in the center of each flower.

With RS facing, sew 14 flowers evenly spaced around the wrist area of each glove.

Rose Headband

This flower headband is a quick and easy project, so it is ideal for beginners. It can be made in a couple of hours and is perfect to keep your ears warm when you don't want to wear a hat.

YARN
Debbie Bliss Cashmerino Aran, 55% merino wool, 33% acrylic, 12% cashmere worsted (aran) yarn, approx 98yd (90m) per 1¾oz (50g) ball:
1 ball each of:
027 Stone (pale grey) (A)
610 Ruby (red) (B)

HOOK AND EQUIPMENT
US size H/8 (5mm) crochet hook
Yarn sewing needle

GAUGE
16 sts x 10 rows over a 4in (10cm) square, working half double crochet using US size H/8 (5mm) hook and Debbie Bliss Cashmerino Aran.

MEASUREMENTS
The headband is 19¼ x 3¾in (49 x 9.5cm), but length is adjustable to fit any head size.

ABBREVIATIONS
See page 27.

For the headband
Using A, make 15ch.
Row 1: 1sc in 2nd ch from hook, 1sc in each ch to end. (14 sts)
Row 2: 2ch, 1hdc in each sc to end.
Row 3: 2ch, 1hdc in each hdc to end.
Row 4: 1ch, 1sc in each hdc to end.
Row 5: 1ch, 1sc in each sc to end.
Rep Rows 2–5 until work measures about 19¼in (49cm) or to fit around head.
Fasten off.

For the gathering strap
Using A, make 11ch.
Row 1: 1hdc in 3rd ch from hook, 1hdc in each ch to end. (9 hdc)
Row 2: 2ch, 1hdc in each hdc to end.
Rep Row 2 six times more.
Fasten off.

For the flower
Using B, make 55ch.
Row 1 (RS): 1dc in 5th ch from hook, *1ch, skip 1 ch, [1dc, 1ch, 1dc] in next ch; rep from * to end of row.
Row 2: 3ch, 5dc in first 1ch sp, *1sc in next 1ch sp, 6dc in next ch sp; rep from *, working last 6dc in last ch sp. (25 shells)

Fasten off, leaving a long tail for sewing flower together.

Making up and finishing
Fold headband in half so short ends meet, with RS together. Using A, join ends together with sc, working 1sc in each st through both layers. Fasten off. Turn RS out and sew in end.

Fold headband gathering strap around the headband so it covers the seam and join the ends together with sc as for the headband seam. Twist strap around so its seam is inside the headband.

To finish flower, thread needle with yarn tail and weave down side of shell to bottom. Roll first shell tightly to form center bud. Make two stitches at base of shell to hold bud in place and roll remaining strip around bud to form rose, securing as you roll by stitching through layers of chains at bottom of rose. Sew rose in position onto headband gathering strap.

Tip

These are so quick to make, you can crochet them in various colors to match your different outfits.

Turban Headband

A really quick and easy project, this headband is ideal for beginners. It can be made in a couple of hours, keeps you warm and is a lot less bulky than a thick hat.

YARN
Debbie Bliss Rialto DK, 100% merino wool light worsted (DK) yarn, approx 115yd (105m) per 1¾oz (50g) ball:
  1 ball of 20 Teal

HOOK AND EQUIPMENT
US size G/6 (4mm) crochet hook
Yarn sewing needle

GAUGE
Gauge is not critical on this project.

MEASUREMENTS
The headband is 19½ x 3¾in (49 x 9.5cm).

ABBREVIATIONS
See page 27.

For the headband
Make 17ch.
Row 1: 1hdc in 2nd ch from hook, 1hdc in each ch to end. (15 sts)
Row 2: 2ch, 1hdc in each st to end.
Rep Row 2 until work measures approx 19½in (49cm) or to fit around head.
Fasten off.

For the front tie
Make 10ch.
Row 1: 1hdc in 2nd ch from hook. (9 sts)
Row 2: 2ch, 1hdc in each st to end.
Rep Row 2 until work measures approx 3½in (9cm).
Fasten off.

Making up and finishing
Fold headband in half so short ends meet, with RS together, and join ends together with ss. Turn RS out.
  Wrap tie around headband and join ends of tie with ss, making sure seam is on WS of headband.

CHAPTER 3

TO *Carry*

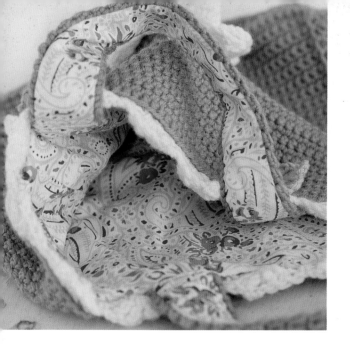

Tote Bag

This is a great size for a bag—it's big enough for essentials or you can use it to store all those balls of yarn. You could omit the fabric lining if you prefer.

Skills needed:
- **Single crochet**
- **Working in rows**
- **Making a single crochet seam**
- **Adding an edging**
- **Joining rounds with a slip stitch**
- **Working into back loop**
- **Working into a chain space**
- **Treble**
- **Working a sequence of stitches into one stitch**
- **Changing color**
- **Double crochet**
- **Double treble**

YARN

Bag:
Debbie Bliss Cashmerino Aran, 55% merino wool, 33% acrylic, 12% cashmere worsted (aran) yarn, approx 98yd (90m) per 1¾oz (50g) ball:
   4 balls of 61 Jade (green) (A)

Edging:
Debbie Bliss Rialto DK, 100% merino wool light worsted (DK) yarn, approx 115yd (105m) per 1¾oz (50g) ball:
   1 ball of 02 Ecru (cream) (B)

Flowers:
Debbie Bliss Baby Cashmerino, 55% wool, 33% acrylic, 12% cashmere sportweight (lightweight DK) yarn, approx 137yd (125m) per 1¾oz (50g) ball:
   Small amounts each of:
   300 Black (C)
   101 Ecru (cream) (D)
   34 Red (E)
   10 Lilac (pale grey-lilac) (F)
   06 Candy Pink (bright pink) (G)
   01 Primrose (yellow) (H)

HOOK AND EQUIPMENT

US size E/4 (3.5mm) and US size G/6 (4mm) crochet hooks
34 x 18in (85 x 45cm) of lining fabric
Sewing needle and matching thread

GAUGE

17 sts x 20 rows over a 4in (10cm) square, working single crochet using US size E/4 (3.5mm) hook and Debbie Bliss Cashmerino Aran.

MEASUREMENTS

The tote bag is 9¾ x 9½ x 4¼in (25 x 23 x 11cm), including top edging.

ABBREVIATIONS

See page 27.

For the tote bag

(make 2, front and back)
Using A and US size E/4 (3.5mm) hook, make 43ch.
Row 1: 1sc in 2nd ch from hook, 1sc in each ch to end of row. (42 sts)
Row 2: 1ch, 1sc in each sc to end. Rep Row 2 until work measures about 8½in (21.5cm).
Fasten off.

For the sides
(make 2)
Using A and US size E/4 (3.5mm) hook, make 18ch.
Row 1: 1sc in 2nd ch from hook, 1sc in each ch to end of row. (17 sts)
Row 2: 1ch, 1sc in each sc to end.
Rep Row 2 until work measures about 8½in (21.5cm) or to match Front/Back.
Fasten off.

For the base
(make 1)
Using A and US size E/4 (3.5mm) hook, make 43ch.
Row 1: 1sc in 2nd ch from hook, 1sc in each ch to end of row. (42 sts)
Row 2: 1ch, 1sc in each sc to end.
Rep Row 2 until work measures about 4¼in (11cm).
Fasten off.

For the handles
(make 2)
Using A and US size E/4 (3.5mm) hook, make 7ch.
Row 1: 1sc in 2nd ch from hook, 1sc in each of next 5 ch. (6 sts)
Rows 2–60: 1ch, 1sc in each sc to end.
Fasten off.

For the edging
With WS together, join side of Front to one edge of first Side with a sc seam using A and US size E/4 (3.5mm) hook. Rep for second Side, then join Back in the same way. With WS together, attach Base to Front, Back and Sides in same way. In Round 1, work into back loops only along sc of top edge.
Round 1 (RS): Using B and US size E/4 (3.5mm) hook, join yarn with a ss in seam at beg of top of Front, make 1ch, 1sc in same place as ss, then counting each sc along top edge as a st (42 sts across Front and Back, 17 sts across each Side) and each seam as a st (4 seams) work as follows—*1ch, skip 1 st, 1sc in next st; rep from * to last st, 1ch, skip 1 st, join with a ss in first sc. (61 ch sps)
Cont with RS facing.
Round 2: 1ch, 1sc in first ch sp, *1ch, skip next ch sp, [2tr, 4ch, 1ss in first of 4ch, 2tr] in next ch sp, 1ch, skip next ch sp, 1sc in next ch sp; rep from * to last 2 ch sps, skip 2 ch sps, join with a ss in first sc.
Fasten off.

For the small flowers
(make 1 each in E, F, G and H)
Using C and US size E/4 (3.5mm) hook, make 4ch, join with a ss in first ch to form a ring.

Round 1 (RS): 1ch, 6sc in ring, break off C, join in D with a ss in first sc. (6 sts)

Cont in rounds with RS always facing.

Round 2: 1ch, 2sc in each st to end, break off D, join in E, F, G or H with a ss in first sc. (12 sts)

Round 3: *3ch, 2tr in next st, 3ch, 1ss in next st; rep from * to end, join with a ss at base of first 3-ch. (6 petals)

Fasten off.

For the large flower
(make 2)

Using C and US size G/6 (4mm), make 4ch, join with a ss in first ch to form a ring.

Round 1 (RS): 1ch, 6sc in ring, break off C, join in G with a ss in first sc. (6 sts)

Cont in rounds with RS always facing.

Round 2: 1ch, 2sc in each st to end, join with a ss in first sc. (12 sts)

Round 3: 1ch, 2sc in each st to end, break off G, join in B with a ss in first sc. (24 sts)

Round 4: *5ch, 1dtr in each of next 3 sts, 5ch, 1ss in next st; rep from * to end, join with a ss at base of first 5-ch. (6 petals)

Fasten off.

For the lining
From the lining fabric cut two pieces 11 x 9¾in (28 x 24.5cm) for front and back, two pieces 5½ x 9¾in (14 x 24.5cm) for sides, one piece 11 x 5½in (28 x 14cm) for base, and two pieces 2½ x 12in (6 x 30cm) for handles (or to fit measurements of crochet bag once made).

With RS together, pin and sew sides to front and back, taking a ⅝in (1.5cm) seam allowance throughout. Press seams open. With RS together, pin and sew base to front, back and sides. Press seams open.

Fold ⅝in (1.5cm) to WS along top edge and press.

Fit lining inside crocheted bag and pin around top edge.

Handles:

Fold ⅝in (1.5cm) to WS along both long sides of the handles and press. Pin lining onto WS of each crocheted handle. Hand sew lining onto each handle, using whip stitch.

Insert one end of handle by about ⅜in (1cm) between lining and crochet piece positioned about 1in (2.5cm) from seam on front and the other end the same distance from the other seam, then pin in place. Rep for other handle on back. Hand sew lining to top of crochet piece, securing the handles in place by stitching twice across the top of each end.

Making up and finishing
Block, starch and press flowers. Sew one small flower at base of each handle end on front and back of bag. Place one large flower on top of the other with petals alternating. Sew onto center front of bag.

Crochet Set Cozy

At home I keep my crochet hooks in jelly pots, but when I go out I like to take a portable crochet hook cozy and this is just the perfect size. It's made in the round, using spirals—and it makes a great gift for someone, with a set of crochet hooks inside.

YARN

Louisa Harding Cassia, 75% superwash wool, 25% nylon light worsted (DK) yarn, approx 144yd (132m) per 1¾oz (50g) ball:
  1 ball each of:
  112 Prince (blue) (A)
  102 Ecru (off white) (B)

HOOK AND EQUIPMENT

US size C/2 (3mm) crochet hook
1 small button

GAUGE

20 sts x 22 rows over 4in (10cm) square, working single crochet using US size C/2 (3mm) hook and Louisa Harding Cassia.

MEASUREMENTS

The hook cozy is 2¼ x 8in (5.5 x 20cm).

ABBREVIATIONS

See page 27.

For the cozy

Using A, make 2ch, 6sc in second ch from hook. Place a stitch marker in loop on hook.

Round 1: 2sc in each st to end. (12 sts)

Round 2: 2sc in each st to end. (24 sts)

Rounds 3–4: 1sc in back loop of each st to end. (24 sts)

Work should now look like a small bowl curving inward. Turn work out so that ridges formed by working in back loops are on outside.

Cont to work on this side of work.

Round 5: Working in both loops of each st, 1sc in each st to end. (24 sts)

Cont working 1sc in each st, in a spiral, until work measures approx 6¾in (17cm) or until piece is same size as length of crochet hooks.

Turn, then begin working in rows.

Next 12 rows: 1ch, 1sc in each of next 13 sts. (13 sts)

Next row: 1ch, sc2tog, 1sc in each of next 9 sts, sc2tog. (11 sts)
Next row: 1ch, 1sc in each st to end. (11 sts)
Next row: 1ch, sc2tog, 1sc in each of next 7 sts, sc2tog. (9 sts)
Next row: 1ch, 1sc in each st to end. (9 sts)
Next row: 1ch, sc2tog, 1sc in each of next 5 sts, sc2tog. (7 sts)

Make buttonhole:
Next row: 1ch, sc2tog, 2ch, skip next 3 sts, sc2tog.
Next row: 1ch, 2sc in ch sp, ss in last st. (4 sts).
Cut yarn, do not fasten off.

Edging:
Join B, 1ch, make approx 21sc down first side, 1sc in each st along front edge, make about 25sc along second side and top to join. Join with a ss in first sc.
Fasten off.

Making up and finishing
Sew in ends, then sew on a button to match the buttonhole.

Floral Purse

This is a really easy and pretty purse to make and a great beginner's project—it takes only a small amount of time to achieve maximum effect. You could omit the fabric lining if you prefer.

Skills needed:

- Single crochet
- Half double crochet
- Working in rows
- Half double crochet 2 stitches together decrease
- Making a buttonhole
- Adding an edging
- Double crochet
- Changing color
- Adding a fabric lining

YARN

Debbie Bliss Cashmerino Aran, 55% merino wool, 33% acrylic, 12% cashmere worsted (aran) yarn, approx 98yd (90m) per 1¾oz (50g) ball:
  1 ball of 011 Green (MC)
  Small lengths of DK yarn in pinks, purples, blues and yellow for flowers

HOOK AND EQUIPMENT

US size 7 (4.5mm) and US size G/6 (4mm) crochet hooks
Yarn sewing needle
10 x 12in (25.5 x 30.5cm) of lining fabric
Sewing needle and thread
1 button, ½in (1cm) in diameter

GAUGE

Gauge is not critical on this project.

MEASUREMENTS

The purse is approx 6 x 4in (15 x 10cm).

ABBREVIATIONS

See page 27.

For the purse

Using MC and US size 7 (4.5mm) crochet hook, make 24ch.
Row 1: 1hdc into second ch from hook, 1hdc in each ch to end, 2ch, turn. (22 sts—2ch counts as first hdc)
Row 2: 1hdc into each st, 2ch, turn. Rep Row 2 until work measures approx 7½in (19cm).

Make flap:
Rows 1–4: 2ch, hdc2tog, 1hdc in each st to end. (18 sts)
Rows 5–7: 2ch, hdc2tog, 1hdc to last 2 sts, hdc2tog. (12 sts)

Make buttonhole:
Row 1: 2ch, hdc2tog, 1hdc in each of next 2 sts, 2ch, skip 2 sts, 1hdc in each of next 3 sts, hdc2tog.
Row 2: 2ch, hdc2tog, 1hdc in next st, 2hdc in ch sp, 1hdc in next 3 sts. (8 sts)

Edging:
Turn and make 32sc sts along first side, 3sc into corner st, 22sc sts along bottom edge, 3sc into corner st, 32sc sts along second side.
Fasten off.

For the flowers

(make 4)

Use two colors for each flower.
Using first color and US size G/6 (4mm) hook, 6ch, join with a ss into first ch.
Make 16sc into circle, joining tail around into each st, join with a ss. Fasten off.
Join second color in fastened-off st. *3ch, make 1dc into next two sts, 3ch, ss into next st; rep from * 4 more times. (5 petals)
Fasten off.
Pull tail to close up center hole and sew in ends.

For the lining

Block crocheted piece. Cut a piece of lining fabric the same size and shape of the purse, plus an extra ⅝in (1.5cm) hem allowance all round. Pin, press and machine or hand sew hems of lining. Match up buttonhole position on crocheted piece and make a buttonhole on lining to correspond.

Making up and finishing

With RS facing upwards, pin lining to WS of crocheted piece. Hand stitch in place, ensuring that the buttonholes match up. With RS of lining facing, turn bottom edge up to start of flap (decrease sides). Using yarn, sew side seams of purse, leaving the flap open. Sew on button to correspond with buttonhole. Sew three flowers to front and one to back of purse.

Patchwork Bag

This bag is made up of simple squares joined together to make a front, back, sides, and bottom. It's a good size and is lined with fabric, with part of the fabric backed with fusible interfacing to add some structure—but you could omit the lining if you prefer.

YARN

Debbie Bliss Rialto DK, 100% merino wool light worsted (DK) yarn, approx 115yd (105m) per 1¾oz (50g) ball:

- 3 balls of 53 Basil (deep green) (MC)
- 1 ball each of:
- 79 Ultra Marine (dark blue)
- 34 Fuchsia (deep pink)
- 12 Scarlet (red)
- 64 Mauve (pink-purple)
- 60 Sky (pale blue)
- 59 Willow (pale green)
- 02 Ecru (cream)

HOOK AND EQUIPMENT

US size G/6 (4mm) crochet hook
Yarn sewing needle
30 x 40in (75 x 100cm) of lining fabric
4 x 36in (10 x 92cm) of fusible interfacing (optional)
Sewing needle and thread

GAUGE

Gauge is not critical on this project.

MEASUREMENTS

The bag is approx 12 x 12in (30 x 30cm).

ABBREVIATIONS

See page 27.

For the squares

(make 27)
Use different color combinations and change color for each round, always using MC for Rounds 4 and 5.
Using first color, 4ch, join with a ss.

Round 1: 3ch (counts as 1dc), 2dc into ring, *1ch, 3dc into ring; rep from * twice more, 1ch, ss into top of first 3-ch.
Fasten off.

Round 2: Join 2nd color into fastened-off st, make ss into each of next 2 dc and next 1ch sp, 3ch, 4dc into same sp to make a corner, *1dc into top center st of next 3-dc group, 5dc into next ch sp to make another corner; rep from * twice more, 1dc into top center st of next 3-dc group, ss to top of 3-ch.
Fasten off.

Round 3: Join 3rd color into top of center st of any corner group, 3ch, 5dc into same place to make corner, *3dc into top st of next single dc, 6dc into top center st of next corner group; rep from * twice, 3dc into top st of next single dc, ss to top of 3-ch. Fasten off.

Round 4: Join MC between 3rd and 4th dc of any corner group, 3ch, 5dc into same place for corner, *3dc in next sp, 3dc in next sp, 6dc into center of next corner group; rep from * twice more, 3dc in next sp, 3dc in next sp, ss to top of 3-ch. Do not fasten off.

Round 5: Cont in MC, 1ch, 1sc in top of next 2 sts, 3sc in next st, *1sc in next 11 sts, 3sc; rep from * twice more, 1sc in next 9 sts, ss to top of first sc. Fasten off.

Making up and finishing

Using a sc seam, attach squares together. Make two panels (front and back) of 3 x 3 squares. Add three squares down each side of one set. Join to other set, leaving one seam open. Join three squares across at the bottom of one set to form the base of the bag. Join these three squares to other panel and base of sides.

For the top edging

Join yarn to any stitch across top edge. Make a sc edging around top: at each of 4 corners, *skip 1 st, ss into next st and continue to make 1sc in each st until next corner. Rep from * for each corner. Fasten off.

For the handles

(make two)
Using MC, make 110ch.
1hdc in 2nd ch from hook, 1hdc in each ch to end.
Fasten off.
Change to next color, 1hdc in each st to end.
Fasten off.
Change to next color, make 1hdc in each st to end.
Fasten off.
Change to MC, make 1hdc in each st to end.
Fasten off.

For the lining

Measure crocheted bag across width and length in several places. (It should be approx 12 x 12in/30.5 x 30.5cm) Add ⅝in (1.5cm) for each side seam and 2in (5cm) for top and bottom and cut 2 pieces of lining to match (approx 13 x 14in/33.5 x 35.5cm) for front and back. Measure down one side of crocheted side panel, along bottom and up second side panel. Add an extra 2in (5cm) for top and bottom and ⅝in (1.5cm) to width for seams and cut one long strip of fabric to match (approx 40 x 5½in/100 x 14cm) for sides and bottom lining.

Measure fusible interfacing against sides and bottom fabric strip and cut to same size. Place fabric RS upward on top of interfacing and press to fuse together. With RS together, pin the strip down one side of the front piece. Sew seam, stopping ⅝in (1.5cm) before bottom corner. Turn corner: make a small cut ⅝in (1.5cm) across and ⅝in (1.5cm) up from first corner of long piece of fabric across seam allowance. Turn fabric strip around corner. Pin next seam (bottom) and sew. Cut long fabric strip at corner as before. Turn around corner, pin strip along last side edge and sew to end. Repeat on other side of sides and bottom strip to join to back piece. Finish seams.

Turn top of lining over to WS by approx 1½in (4cm), so lining fits inside top edge of bag without showing above crocheted piece. Place lining in bag and pin top edge of lining to top edge of crocheted piece.

Measure crocheted handles, add ⅝in (1.5cm) to each side and both ends and cut two strips of lining fabric to this length (each approx 28 x 2½in/71 x 6.5cm). Pin and press lining to fit just on inside of handle pieces. Hand sew in place.

To attach handles

Handles should be attached in center of first and last square of front and back of bag. Place a pin 1½in (4cm) from outside edge of each side panel of bag as a marker. With handle lining facing inwards, attach ends of handles approx 2in (5cm) down into bag, aligning outside edge of handle with the pin marker. Hand stitch handles in place, using MC yarn, so that they are sandwiched between lining and crocheted piece. Repeat on same side with other end of same handle. Repeat for second handle on other side of the bag.

Using sewing thread, hand stitch lining to crochet bag around top edge, incorporating handles. Work a few stitches in each corner along bottom and sides to secure lining in position.

Rose Shopper

This easy, quick project, using single crochet throughout, is perfect as a shopper. The lining makes it stronger, but if you are not so handy at sewing it still works brilliantly without one. The flowers are a bit more difficult, so if these are above your skill, replace with some simple flowers from the Floral Purse—see page 78.

Skills needed:
- **Single crochet**
- **Working in rows**
- **Adding an edging**
- **Joining rounds with a slip stitch**
- **Working into a ring**
- **Double crochet**
- **Working into a chain space**
- **Changing color**

YARN
Debbie Bliss Paloma, 60% baby alpaca, 40% merino wool bulky (super chunky) yarn, approx 71yd (65m) per 1¾oz (50g) ball:
  6 balls of:
  44 Robin Egg (pale blue-grey) (A)
  1 ball of:
  26 Lime (green) (B)

Debbie Bliss Cashmerino Aran, 55% merino wool, 33% acrylic, 12% cashmere worsted (aran) yarn, approx 98yd (90m) per 1¾oz (50g) ball:
  1 ball each of:
  73 Coral (orange) (C)
  75 Citrus (green) (D)

HOOK AND EQUIPMENT
US size M/13 (9mm), US size K10½ (7mm), and US size 7 (4.5mm) crochet hooks
Yarn sewing needle
40in (1m) length of lining fabric for bag

28 x 5in (72 x 15cm) of lining fabric for handles
Sewing needle and thread
1 large press stud

GAUGE
Gauge is not critical on this project.

MEASUREMENTS
The shopper is approx 13½ x 11½in (34 x 29cm), with 25in (64cm) long handles.

ABBREVIATIONS
See page 27.

For the main bag
(make 2, front and back)
Using A and US size M/13 (9mm) hook, make 25ch.
Next row: 1ch, 1sc to end.
Rep this row until bag measures 12½in (32cm).
Fasten off.

For the handles

(make two)

Using A and US size K10½ (7mm) hook, make 5ch, turn, 1sc in second ch from hook, 1sc to end. (4 sts)

Next row: 1ch, 1sc in each st to end. (4 sts)

Rep this row until handle measures approx 26in (66cm). Fasten off.

For the flowers

(make 4)

Using C and US size 7 (4.5mm) hook, make 4ch, ss into first ch to make a ring.

Round 1: *1sc, 1dc, 1sc into ring; rep from * 3 more times. (4 petals)

Round 2: *2ch, from WS ss in base of second sc of next petal (pick up 2 loops); rep from * 3 more times. Slip last st into first ss. (4 loops)

Round 3: *4dc into next 2-ch sp, ss into same ch sp; rep from * 3 more times.

Fasten off.

Round 4: Cont working with same color. Work into back of petals and picking up 2 loops, join yarn at base of highest point of previous round, *3ch, ss into middle of base of next petal; rep from * 3 more times, slip last st into joining st.

Round 5: *8dc into next 3-ch sp, ss into next 3-ch sp; rep from * 3 more times, slip last st into joining st.

Fasten off.

Change to D.

Round 6: Working into back of petals and picking up 2 loops, join yarn into middle of base of petal (next 8-dc) of previous round, *3ch, ss into middle of base of next petal; rep from * 3 more times, slip last st into joining st.

Round 7: *10dc into 3-ch sp, ss into same 3-ch sp; rep from * 3 more times.

Fasten off.

Making up and finishing

With WS facing, join front and back by sewing up side and bottom seams, leaving top open. Sew each flower at each handle point at top of bag.

For the edging

Work around top edge of bag. With RS facing and using B and US size M/13 (9mm) hook, join yarn in a corner st, *3ch, ss into third ch from hook, skip 1 st, 1sc into next st; rep from * to end. Ss into joining st.

Fasten off.

For the lining

Measure straps and cut out handle lining same size as crocheted handle, allowing ⅝in (1.5cm) extra for each hem at the sides, top and bottom. With WS facing, press, pin and machine stitch hem of lining along both sides. Press. Place lining on crocheted handle, with WS facing crochet. Pin and hand stitch lining and crocheted handle together. Rep for second handle.

Place a pin 1in (2.5cm) from each outside seam of bag as a marker. With handle lining facing inwards, attach ends of handles approx 2in (5cm) down into bag, aligning outside edge of handle with the pin marker. Hand stitch handles to main piece. Rep on same side with other end of same handle. Rep for second handle on other side of bag.

Cut two pieces of lining fabric to same size as bag, adding ⅝in (1.5cm) seam allowance to sides and base and 1in (2.5cm) to top. With RS together, pin and machine stitch side and bottom seams. Trim bottom corners and press open seams. Turn lining RS out. Turn top edge over to WS by 1in (2.5cm) and press. Insert lining in bag and pin in place around top. Hand stitch lining to main piece around top edge, incorporating handle ends between layers. Sew large press stud on inside center of lining.

Poppy Purse

This pretty purse could be used for money, but also for make-up—or even your crochet hooks and scissors. You could omit the fabric lining if you prefer.

● ●

Skills needed:
- **Single crochet**
- **Working in rows**
- **Single crochet 2 stitches together decrease**
- **Making a buttonhole**
- **Adding an edging**
- **Joining rounds with a slip stitch**
- **Working a half double crochet cluster**
- **Working into a ring**
- **Working into back loop**
- **Treble**
- **Adding a fabric lining**

YARN
Rooster Almerino Aran, 50% baby alpaca, 50% merino wool worsted (aran) yarn, approx 103yd (94m) per 1¾oz (50g) ball:
  1 x ball of 305 Custard (A)

Small amounts of light worsted (DK) yarn in:
  black (B)
  red (C)
  green (D)

HOOK AND EQUIPMENT
US size 7 (4.5mm) and US size E/4 (3.5mm) crochet hooks
Yarn sewing needle
10 x 14in (25.5 x 35.5cm) piece of lining fabric
Sewing needle and matching thread
1 button, ¾in (2cm) in diameter

GAUGE
15½ sts x 18 rows over a 4in (10cm) square, working single crochet using US size 7 (4.5mm) hook and Rooster Almerino Aran.

MEASUREMENTS
The purse is approx 6 x 4in (15 x 10cm).

NOTE
hdcCL = half double crochet cluster. See page 21 for instructions.

ABBREVIATIONS
See page 27.

For the purse

Using A and US size 7 (4.5mm) hook, make 24ch.

Row 1: 1sc in 2nd ch from hook, 1sc in each ch to end. (23 sts)

Row 2: 1ch, 1sc in each st. (23 sts) Rep Row 2 until work measures approx 7½in (19cm).

Make flap:

Rows 1–8: 1ch, sc2tog, 1sc in each st to end. (15 sts)

Row 9: 1ch, sc2tog, 1sc in each of next 4 sts, sc2tog, 1sc in each of next 5 sts, sc2tog. (12 sts)

Make buttonhole:

Row 1: 1ch, sc2tog, 1sc in each of next 3 sts, 2ch, skip 2 sts, 1sc in each of next 3 sts, sc2tog.

Row 2 (RS): 1ch, sc2tog, 1sc in each of next 2 sts, 2sc in 2ch sp, 1sc in each of next 2 sts, sc2tog. (8 sts) Do not fasten off.

Edging:

1ch, work 44sc evenly along one side edge, 3sc in corner st (47 sts), 22sc along bottom edge (69 sts), 3sc in corner st (72 sts), 44sc along second side edge (116 sts), 3sc in corner st (119 sts), 8sc along top edge (127 sts), join with ss in first 1-ch.

Fasten off.

For the poppies

(make 2)

Using B and US size E/4 (3.5mm) hook and leaving a long tail, make 6ch, join with a ss in first ch to form a ring.

Round 1: 2ch, [1hdcCL in ring, 1ch] 12 times, join with a ss in back loop of top of first hdcCL. (12 hdcCL)

Break off B, but do not fasten off.

Round 2: Working in back loops of sts only, join in C, 3ch (counts as 1sc, 2ch), 1sc in top of next hdcCL from previous round, *2ch, 1sc in top of next hdcCL; rep from * to end of round, ending 2ch, join with a ss in first of 3-ch. (12 sc)

Round 3: Working in back loops of sts only, *4ch (counts as first tr), [1tr in each of next 2 ch, 1tr in next sc] 3 times, 1tr in each of next 2 ch, 4ch (counts as 1tr), 1ss in base of last tr, 1ss in next sc (13 tr, 1 petal made); rep from * twice more, working last ss in base of first 4-ch of first petal. (3 petals made)

Fasten off.

Weave B yarn tail around center hole, pull to close and secure. Neaten petals as you sew in remaining ends.

For the lining

Block crocheted piece. Cut a piece of lining fabric the same size and shape as purse allowing an extra ⅝in (1.5cm) seam allowance all around. Fold under the seam allowances all around the lining piece, then pin, press and machine or hand sew in place. Make a buttonhole on lining to correspond with buttonhole position on crocheted piece.

Making up and finishing

With WS together, pin lining onto crocheted piece. Hand sew lining in place, making sure buttonhole positions match. With RS of lining facing, turn up bottom edge to align with start of flap shaping. Using a length of yarn, sew side seams of purse, leaving flap open.

Sew on button to correspond with buttonhole.

Attach one poppy to center of front flap and one poppy to top left-hand corner on back of purse. Using D, embroider a stalk for each poppy in chain stitch.

Kindle Cover

I made this for a Paperwhite Kindle, but the pattern can easily be adjusted to make a cover for any device, including a cellphone, tablet, or laptop. You could omit the fabric lining if you prefer.

Skills needed:

- **Single crochet**
- **Working in rows**
- **Joining rounds with a slip stitch**
- **Working into a ring**
- **Adding a fabric lining**

YARN

Cover:

Debbie Bliss Baby Cashmerino, 55% wool, 33% acrylic, 12% cashmere sportweight (lightweight DK) yarn, approx 137yd (125m) per 1¾oz (50g) ball:

  1 ball of 97 Speedwell (lavender) (MC)

Flowers and leaves:

Scraps of yarn (of same weight as MC) in:

  red (A)
  bright pink (B)
  white (C)
  green (D)

HOOK AND EQUIPMENT

US size C/2 (3mm) crochet hook
8¼ x 13in (21 x 33cm) of lining fabric

Yarn sewing needle
Sewing needle and thread to match lining
32in (80cm) red ribbon, ⅝in (1.5cm) wide

GAUGE

22 sts x 25 rows over a 4in (10cm) square, working single crochet using US size C/2 (3mm) hook and Debbie Bliss Baby Cashmerino.

MEASUREMENTS

The cover is approx 7 x 5¼in (18 x 13.5cm), to fit a Kindle device measuring approx 6¾ x 4¾ x ⅜in (17 x 11.7 x 0.9cm).

NOTES

If your device is a different size, use the gauge as a guide to make a base chain to its width, then continue working Row 2 until the length matches the length of your device.

  If your device is much bigger than 6¾ x 4¾ x ⅜in (17 x 11.7 x 0.9cm) you will need more yarn.

ABBREVIATIONS

See page 27.

For the cover

(make 2, front and back)
Using MC, make 31ch.
Row 1: 1sc in 2nd ch from hook, 1sc in each ch to end. (30 sts)
Row 2: 1ch (does NOT count as a st), 1sc in each sc to end. (30 sts)
Rep Row 2 until work measures 7in (18cm).
Fasten off.

For the flowers

(make 1 in each of A, B and C)
Make 4ch, join with a ss in first ch to form a ring.
Round 1 (RS): [5ch, 1ss in ring] 5 times. (5 petals)
Fasten off.

For the leaves

(make 1 in D)
Make 8ch, join with a ss in first ch to form a ring.
Round 1 (RS): [6ch, 1sc in 2nd ch from hook, 1sc in each of next 4 ch, 1ss in ring] 4 times. (4 leaves)
Fasten off.

For the lining

Cut the lining fabric into two pieces, each 8¼ x 6½in (21 x 16.5cm). If the cover is for a different device, measure the length, width and depth to determine the length and width of the finished cover. Then add another 1⅜in (3.5cm) to both dimensions and cut two pieces of lining fabric to these measurements.

Place the lining pieces RS together and pin along sides and bottom edges. Sew the sides and bottom with a ⅝in (1.5cm) seam.

Press seams open.
Fold ⅝in (1.5cm) to WS along top edge and press.

Making up and finishing

Block and steam front and back to make them the same size. Block the leaves, grouping them to one side of the ring. Sew in all ends.

Place the front and back crochet pieces RS together and join side and bottom seams using MC and

yarn sewing needle. Turn RS out. Place the lining inside the crochet piece, WS together. Pin and hand sew the top edge of the lining to the top edge of the crochet piece using a sewing needle and a matching color thread.

Sew the leaves and then the flowers onto the front of the cover. Cut the ribbon in half and sew one end in the center of the top edge of the lining on either side.

Striped Cellphone Cozy

Skills needed:

- **Single crochet**
- **Working in rows**
- **Changing color**
- **Joining rounds with a slip stitch**
- **Double crochet**

This cozy fits a larger cellphone, and is nice and bright, and easy to find in a bag! Here I've used Baby Cashmerino yarn as I love the colors, but this is a perfect project for using up scraps as it requires very little yarn.

YARN
Debbie Bliss Baby Cashmerino, 55% merino wool, 33% acrylic, 12% cashmere lightweight DK (sport weight) yarn, approx 137yd (125m) per 1¾oz (50g) ball:

1 ball each of:
68 Peach Melba (peach) (A)
59 Mallard (dark blue) (B)
02 Apple (light green) (C)
101 Ecru (off white) (D)
06 Candy Pink (pink) (E)
202 Light Blue (light blue) (F)
34 Red (G)
90 Leaf (dark green) (H)

HOOK AND EQUIPMENT
US size C/2 (3mm) crochet hook
Yarn sewing needle

GAUGE
20 sts x 24 rows over a 4in (10cm) square, working single crochet using US size C/2 (3mm) hook and Debbie Bliss Baby Cashmerino.

MEASUREMENTS
The cover is approx 3½ x 6in (9 x 15cm), to fit a Samsung S5 mobile phone, but you can make it any size.

ABBREVIATIONS
See page 27.

For the cozy
This is made in one piece.
Make 1-row stripes using A, B, C, D, E, F, G, H, changing color on each row.
Row 1: Using any color make 21ch, 1sc in second ch from hook and each ch to end. (20 sts)
Cut yarn, do not fasten off.
Row 2: Join next color, 1ch, 1sc in each st to end. (20 sts)
Cut yarn, do not fasten off.
Rep Row 2 until 72 rows have been worked or to required length.
Fasten off.
Sew in ends.

For the bow
(make one)
Using D, make 16ch, join with a ss to form a ring.
Round 1 (RS): 1ch (does not count as a st), 1sc in each ch to end, join with a ss in first sc. (16 sts)
Round 2: 3ch (counts as dc), 1dc in each st to end; join with a ss in top of first 3-ch. (16 sts)
Round 3: 1ch, 1sc in each st to end, join with a ss in first sc.

Fasten off leaving a tail of approx 17½in (45cm).

Making up and finishing
With RS together, fold cozy in half lengthways and sew up side seams. Block and press.

Turn bow RS out and hold flat, with fasten off st and tail at the top at the front center. Using yarn tail, wrap yarn around center of ring tightly to create bow shape, then secure in place on one side of cozy approx 6 rows from the top, using a yarn sewing needle.

Suppliers

US STOCKISTS

Knitting Fever
(Debbie Bliss yarns)
Stores nationwide
www.knittingfever.com

The Knitting Garden
(Debbie Bliss yarns)
www.theknittinggarden.org

Webs
(yarn, crochet hooks, accessories,
tuition)
75 Service Center Rd
Northampton, MA 01060
1-800-367-9327
www.yarn.com
customerservice@yarn.com

ACCESSORIES
A.C. Moore
(crochet hooks, accessories)
Online and east coast stores
1-888-226-6673
www.acmoore.com

Hobby Lobby
(crochet hooks, accessories)
Online and stores nationwide
1-800-888-0321
www.hobbylobby.com

Jo-Ann Fabric and Craft Store
(crochet hooks, accessories)
Stores nationwide
1-888-739-4120
www.joann.com

Michaels
(crochet hooks, beads)
Stores nationwide
1-800-642-4235
www.michaels.com

UK STOCKISTS

Deramores
(yarn, crochet hooks, accessories)
0845 519 4573 or 01795 668144
www.deramores.com
customer.service@deramores.com

Designer Yarns
(distributor for Debbie Bliss yarns)
www.designeryarns.uk.com

Fyberspates Ltd
(yarn, crochet hooks)
01244 346653
fyberspates@btinternet.com
www.fyberspates.co.uk

Hobbycraft
(yarn, crochet hooks)
Stores nationwide
0330 026 1400
www.hobbycraft.co.uk

Laughing Hens
(yarn, accessories)
The Croft Stables
Station Lane
Great Barrow
Cheshire CH3 7JN
01829 740903
www.laughinghens.com
sales@laughinghens.com

John Lewis
(yarn, crochet hooks, accessories)
Stores nationwide
03456 049049
www.johnlewis.com

TUITION
Nicki Trench
Crochet Club, workshops,
accessories
www.nickitrench.com
nicki@nickitrench.com

ACCESSORIES
Addi Needles
(crochet hooks)
01529 240510
www.addineedles.co.uk
addineedles@yahoo.co.uk

Knit Pro
(crochet hooks)
www.knitpro.eu

Index

Acknowledgments

Thank you to all the CICO Books team, particularly Penny Craig and Marie Clayton for putting together this lovely collection of patterns.

These patterns have been taken from a variety of my crochet books and I'm extremely lucky to have a great team of crocheters and checkers who have worked with me on all the books these patterns are taken from—thank you—you know who you are. A big thanks particularly to Jane Czaja, our current pattern checker for her meticulous attention to detail.

It's very important for me to have good quality yarns in beautiful colors and special thanks to Designer Yarns for providing most of the yarns in these patterns, and thanks particularly to Graeme Knowles-Miller for being so efficient and quick at sorting out the yarns for me. Also thanks to Jeni Brown at Fyberspates.

And thanks to the team of photographers, stylists and layout designers who always manage to do us all proud.